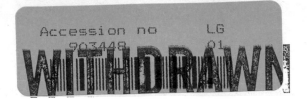

KING LEAR

By the same author

Citizen Comedy in the Age of Shakespeare (University of
    Toronto Press, 1973)
Shakespeare's Comedy of Love (Methuen, 1974)
Ben Jonson: His Vision and his Art (Methuen, 1981)
English Drama: Shakespeare to the Restoration, 1590–1660
    (Longman, 1988)
Shakespeare's Political Drama (Routledge, 1988)

Harvester New Critical Introductions to Shakespeare

KING LEAR

Alexander Leggatt

Professor of English, University College,
University of Toronto

HARVESTER · WHEATSHEAF
NEW YORK LONDON TORONTO SYDNEY TOKYO

First published 1988 by
Harvester · Wheatsheaf
66 Wood Lane End, Hemel Hempstead,
Hertfordshire HP2 4RG

A division of Simon & Schuster International Group

Typeset in 11/12 point Goudy Old Style by C. R.
Barber & Partners (Highlands) Ltd, Fort William,
Scotland

Printed and bound in Great Britain by
Billing and Sons Ltd, Worcester

British Library Cataloguing in Publication Data

Leggatt, Alexander
King Lear.—(Harvester new critical
introductions to Shakespeare).
1. Shakespeare, William. King Lear
I. Title   II. Shakespeare, William. King Lear
822.3'3   PR2819

ISBN 0-7108-1111-X
ISBN 0-7108-0919-0 Pbk

1 2 3 4 5   92 91 90 89 88

For my daughters

Titles in the Series

GENERAL EDITOR: GRAHAM BRADSHAW

General Editor's Preface

The *New Critical Introductions to Shakespeare* series will include studies of all Shakespeare's plays, together with two volumes on the non-dramatic verse, and is designed to offer a challenge to all students of Shakespeare.

Each volume will be brief enough to read in an evening, but long enough to avoid those constraints which are inevitable in articles and short essays. Each contributor will develop a sustained critical reading of the play in question, which addresses those difficulties and critical disagreements which each play has generated.

Different plays present different problems, different challenges and excitements. In isolating these, each volume will present a preliminary survey of the play's stage history and critical reception. The volumes then provide a more extended discussion of these matters in the main text, and of matters relating to genre, textual problems and the use of source material, or to historical and theoretical issues. But here, rather than setting a row of dragons at the gate, we have assumed that 'background' should figure only as it emerges into a critical foreground; part of the critical endeavour is to establish, and sift, those issues which seem most pressing.

So, for example, when Shakespeare determined that *his* Othello and Desdemona should have no time to live together, or that Cordelia dies while Hermione survives, his deliberate departures from his source material have a critical significance which is often blurred, when discussed in the context of lengthily detailed surveys of 'the sources'. Alternatively, plays like *The Merchant of Venice* or *Measure for Measure* show Shakespeare welding together different 'stories' from quite different sources, so that their relation to each other becomes a matter for critical debate. And Shakespeare's dramatic practice poses different critical questions when we ask—or if we ask: few do—why particular characters in a poetic drama speak only in verse or only in prose; or when we try to engage with those recent, dauntingly specialised and controversial textual studies which set out to establish the evidence for authorial revisions or joint authorship. We all read *King Lear* and *Macbeth*, but we are not all textual critics; nor are textual critics always able to show where their arguments have critical consequences which concern us all.

Just as we are not all textual critics, we are not all linguists, cultural anthropologists, psychoanalysts or New Historicists. The diversity of contemporary approaches to Shakespeare is unprecedented, enriching, bewildering. One aim of this series is to represent what is illuminating in this diversity. As the hastiest glance through the list of contributors will confirm, the series does not attempt to 're-read' Shakespeare by placing an ideological grid over the text and reporting on whatever shows through. Nor would the series' contributors always agree with each other's arguments, or premises; but each has been invited to develop a sustained critical argument which will also provide its own critical and historical context—by taking account of those issues which have perplexed or divided audiences, readers, and critics past and present.

Graham Bradshaw

Contents

Preface

In the twentieth century *King Lear* has replaced *Hamlet* as the play most commonly considered Shakespeare's masterpiece. Such shifts in judgement are a sign of how much the critical reception of a Shakespeare play (as of any work of art) depends on cultural factors that change over the years. The untidiness of the play's story-telling and the cruelty of its vision were stumbling blocks for earlier generations, but bring the play close to our own time. An age that has absorbed the paintings of Picasso and the music of Stravinsky is not likely to be puzzled by the twisted shapes and discords of *King Lear*. While the eighteenth century, for example, found in the play the pathos of a wronged old man, we are more inclined to look at the toughness and violence of its larger vision. Previous generations of critics found the blinding of Gloucester revolting and excused its presence in the play on the grounds of its thematic importance. Now anyone who receives reports from Amnesty International knows that Shakespeare is simply telling us what the world is like, in our time as in his. And it is in our time that the play has finally come into its own in the theatre. Expecting neat construction and realistic staging, the theatre of the period up to the Great War was uncomfortable with *King Lear*. Freer staging conventions, and reactions against theatrical realism, have allowed the play to emerge as a natural stage piece.

The bleakness of *King Lear*, its refusal to tell its story conventionally, and its inherent theatricality are all issues to which we will return in the pages that follow. But the truism that the play presents different faces to different generations has an especially interesting application in the area of textual studies, and this question should be dealt with now. *King Lear* was first printed in 1608, in the so-called 'Quarto' text, one of a number of play texts that appeared in Shakespeare's lifetime, apparently without his authorisation. It appeared next in the 'Folio' of 1623, the collected edition of Shakespeare's works compiled after his death by two of his fellow actors. The two versions of the play are different at many points, and the differences are not just small variations in language but matters that affect character, story-line and structure. Each text contains material not found in the other. Until recently, editions of *King Lear* were based on the assumption that the Quarto and the Folio were imperfect reports of a single lost Shakespearean original that could be reproduced (approximately at least) by combining them. The result has been a so-called 'conflated' text based usually on the Folio but combining all the available material from both versions, and producing a third version longer than either.

This is the text that most of us are used to. But in the last ten years a number of scholars have argued that the Quarto and Folio represent different stages in Shakespeare's own revision of the play, and that while the Folio is later and generally better, each text has its own integrity. The 'conflated' text, on the other hand, goes against Shakespeare's intentions by combining material that was never meant to be combined, and produces a new play that is to a dangerous extent an editor's invention. The matter is still hotly debated; but a number of scholars (including the present author) are now persuaded that the two-text theory is sufficently plausible that any responsible reading of the

play must take it into account. It clears up a number of small
confusions, and the Folio in particular emerges as a tight,
economical stage piece with a swiftness of attack that seems
more in keeping with the spirit of the play than the slower,
more ponderous conflated text. At the time of writing, the
only readily available edition that prints the two texts is
William Shakespeare, The Complete Works, edited by Stanley
Wells and Gary Taylor (Clarendon Press, Oxford, 1986);
accordingly, this is the edition I have used. My discussion is
based on the Folio text (called in the Oxford edition *The
Tragedy of King Lear*) and act, scene and line references are to
that text. I have referred occasionally to the Quarto text
(called in Oxford *The History of King Lear*—the titles reflect
the titles in the original editions). Such passages are
identified by the letter 'Q' and are followed by scene and line
numbers; there are no act divisions in the Quarto text.
Readers who are following my discussion using other
editions should not find many difficulties, for the conflated
text is generally based on the Folio and the most important
changes in Oxford are cuts. (However, in parts of Acts 2 and
4 the Oxford scene numbering is different from that in most
editions, and I have given the traditional scene numbers in
square brackets for the convenience of readers with other
texts.) Fortunately, the central critical questions are the
same whatever text one is using. When the detailed changes
are significant I have called attention to them.

It is appropriate that the text of *King Lear* should present
a problem, and challenge, of this kind, and that the most
recent thinking in textual scholarship should have brought
this problem to light. For us, knowledge is shifting and
relative; we no longer see texts as fixed, unchanging
documents. Even for its author, *King Lear* seems to have
resisted being locked into a single form. And what the
present discussion will emphasise is that for us, too, as
readers and audiences, *King Lear* is a dynamic play, a play
that refuses to sit still.

Acknowledgements

I am grateful to Graham Bradshaw and Sue Roe for their guidance and advice at every stage of this project.

The Stage History

In Shakespeare's time plays were regularly presented at court during the Christmas season, and the first recorded performance of *King Lear* took place there on 26 December 1606. It had presumably been in the repertory of Shakespeare's company, the King's Men, for some weeks or months before that. Though an elegy on the company's leading actor, Richard Burbage, mentions 'kind Lear' as one of his notable roles, the relatively small number of references to the play throughout the seventeenth century leads one to conjecture that it was not one of Shakespeare's more popular works. In 1681 Nahum Tate's version, with a happy ending in which Lear is restored, the Fool is cut, and Cordelia marries Edgar, effectively banished Shakepeare's play from the stage for around 150 years. The noted actors of the period, such as Betterton, Quin and John Philip Kemble, used this version or variations of it. The greatest of these actors was David Garrick, who, appealing to the sentimental taste of his time, moved audiences to tears with his portrayal of Lear as a wronged old man. When in 1808 Charles Lamb declared the play unstageable since the theatre could show only 'an old man trottering about the stage with a walking stick', he could point to the fact that the theatre had solved the problem by preferring Tate to Shakespeare. He was also expressing the Romantic

preference for a grand, titanic Lear, a preference that has
lasted well into our own time, and that raises expectations
hard for the theatre to satisfy. In the nineteenth century only
William Charles Macready came close to success. His 1838
production replaced Tate, if not with Shakespeare's text, at
least with a trimmed and bowdlerized version of it suitable
for Victorian taste. Macready himself had something like
the emotional power and scale the role was thought to
require. But other great actors of the period failed, in
varying degrees: Edmund Kean's Lear was only fitfully
powerful, Samuel Phelps's was sentimental, Edwin Booth's
was compared to Polonius, and Henry Irving's, after a
strong initial entrance, lapsed into feebleness. In 1904 A.C.
Bradley could still describe the play as 'too huge for the
stage'.

In the twentieth century this judgement has been
decisively overturned. Though productions through to the
1950s continued to use the realistic scenery conventional to
the time, thereby robbing the staging of the Elizabethan
freedom it needs, a number of notable actors rose to the
challenge of the central part. Chief among these was John
Gielgud, who played the role at various times from 1931 to
1955, most notably at the Old Vic in 1940 in a production
whose key rehearsals were conducted by Harley Granville-
Barker. Gielgud's emotional power and mastery of
Shakespeare's language made him, for many audience
members, the greatest Lear they had seen. Donald Wolfit, in
his own touring production, was also praised for the
emotional power of his best performances, though the effect
was vitiated by a shabby production and an inadequate
supporting cast. Laurence Olivier (Old Vic, 1946; directed
by Oliver himself) combined pride with a dotty, eccentric
comedy for which he was criticised in some quarters.
Michael Redgrave (Stratford upon Avon, 1953; directed by
George Devine) was majestic, and especially effective in the
mad scenes. The tradition of a softer and more human Lear
persisted in controversial performances by Charles

Laughton (Stratford upon Avon, 1953; directed by Glen Byam Shaw) and Peter Ustinov (Stratford, Ontario, 1979). The latter was the centre of an imaginative production by Robin Phillips, which set the play in the nineteenth century and gave it a strongly military flavour. Donald Sinden's 1976 Lear for the Royal Shakespeare Company, (directed by Trevor Nunn, John Barton and Barry Kyle) also in a Victorian setting, was more traditionally majestic.

The major turning point for *King Lear* on the modern stage was Peter Brook's 1962 production for the Royal Shakespeare Company, with Paul Scofield as a tough, abrasive Lear. Brook's stylised staging, indebted both to Brecht and to Oriental theatre, broke the old pictorial mold—realistic sets were replaced by plain, movable white walls—and his bleak, pessimistic reading (influenced by Jan Kott's *Shakespeare Our Contemporary*) linked the play to the then-fashionable Theatre of the Absurd. The production was especially well received in Eastern Europe, where it was thought to capture the anxieties of the post-war world. Its pesimistic slanting of the play (created partly by cuts in the text) roused controversy, and continues to do so. Adrian Noble's 1982 Royal Shakespeare Company production, less abstract than Brook's, used more explicitly modern images to evoke the play's harshness; it was notable for a robust Lear by Michael Gambon and a red-nosed circus clown of a Fool by Antony Sher. American actors tackling the part have generally been criticised for lacking tragic grandeur, but Morris Carnovsky, whose 1963 performance at Stratford, Connecticut (directed by Allen Fletcher) was praised for its humanity and emotional power, was an exception.

The play is available in several screen versions. Grigori Kozintsev's 1970 film uses the Russian landscape to create a vast, windswept setting and makes the common people an active presence. His leading actor, Yari Yarvet, small, beardless and excitable, breaks with the tradition of physically imposing Lears. Peter Brook's 1971 film, again with Paul Scofield, recreates the bleakness of his stage version in cinematic terms. Two sharply contrasting television versions are available: in the BBC Shakespeare production (1982; directed by Jonathan Miller) Michael Horden's Lear is a low-key, realistic study in senility, acted against an almost featureless background. Laurence Olivier's version (Granada TV, 1983; directed by Michael Elliott), on the other hand, sets the play with elaborate detail in Druid Britain, and Oliver's own performance is bold as well as poignant.

The present discussion will refer to actual productions only occasionally; but the issues raised by Tate's sentimentalizing of the play and by Brook's pessimistic reading will be among our central concerns, as will the challenge posed by Lamb and Bradley to the play's theatrical viablility.

The Critical Reception

Early reactions, including the comments of Samuel Johnson in his 1765 edition, Coleridge's jottings and Keats's sonnet 'On Sitting Down to Read *King Lear* Once Again', have suggested the play's unusual and disturbing power. But it is A.C. Bradley, in his influential *Shakespearean Tragedy* (1904), who sets the agenda for twentieth-century criticism, with his reading of the play as the story of Lear's education and redemption, and his insistence that it is imperfect as a stage piece. Bradley's claim for Lear's redemption produces a reading that, while acknowledging the play's horror, is in the last analysis positive and optimistic. His lead has been followed to varying degrees by G. Wilson Knight in *The Wheel of Fire* (1930), Derek A. Traversi in *An Approach to Shakespeare* (1938) and L.C. Knights in *Some Shakespearean Themes* (1959). The case is put in its most extreme form by Irving Ribner in *Patterns in Shakespearian Tragedy* (1960). Bradley's lead is also followed by Paul A. Jorgensen, who in *Lear's Self-Discovery* (1967) attributes greater intelligence to Lear than most critics do, and by Robert Bechtold Heilman, whose *This Great Stage* (1948), a magisterial study of the play's structure and imagery, is perhaps the fullest critical statement that the play is coherent, ordered and affirmative.

The positive reading of the play is sometimes labelled 'Christian'. While it is generally agreed that Shakespeare took the story's pre-Christian setting quite seriously, denying his characters any knowledge of Christian revelation, the values the positive readings affirm are Christian ones, and this sometimes carries the implication that Christian faith underlies the play. The most elaborate counter-argument is found in William R. Elton's *King Lear and the Gods* (1966), which places *King Lear* against the religious thinking of Shakespeare's time, and emphasises the play's scepticism. A brief but trenchant attack on the 'Christian' interpretation is Barabara Everett's article 'The New King Lear', *Critical Quarterly* 2 (1960), which disputes the reading of Lear as educated and redeemed, taking aim particularly at Kenneth Muir's Arden edition (1952). Jan Kott's absurdist reading 'King Lear, or Endgame' (1961), reprinted in his *Shakespeare Our Contemporary* (1964), had considerable impact when it first appeared and influenced Peter Brook's famous stage production; but the impact has since faded. More recent studies such as S.L. Goldberg's *An Essay on King Lear* (1974) and Stephen Booth's *King Lear, Macbeth, Indefinition and Tragedy* (1983), have emphasised the play's open, tentative quality, its tendency not to affirm but to surprise our expectations and qualify our readings.

The Christian reading, pronouned dead by some critics, has been revived by others. Walter Stein in *Criticism as Dialogue* (1969) sees an implied affirmation in the sheer relentlessness with which the play faces despair, and Harold Skulsky in *Spirits Finely Touched* (1976) uses the kind of background to which Elton appealed but disputes his conclusions. On the other hand, the positive values affirmed even in the more sceptical humanist readings are countered by a number of recent critics who shift their emphasis away from kindness and forgiveness and on to politics. Jonathan Dollimore, in *Radical Tragedy* (1984), sees the play not only as refusing closure but as taking for its principal themes power, property and class. For David Pirie, in 'Lear as King', *Critical Quarterly* 22 (1980), the issue is Lear's political role, and his reunion with Cordelia brings not redemption but disaster, leading Lear to a total neglect of his public responsibilities. In her feminist critique of the play, 'The Patriarchal Bard: Feminist Criticism and Shakespeare: *King Lear* and *Measure for Measure*', in *Political Shakespeare*, edited by Jonathan Dollimore and Alan Sinfield (1985), Kathleen McLuskie notes that the play's emotional impact is inevitably bound up with its acceptance of a patriarchal order, but argues that the play also contains material a feminist critic may use in subverting the values of that order.

The play's theatricality, denied by Bradley, was defended by an experienced actor and producer, Harley Granville-Barker, in his *Prefaces to Shakespeare* (1946). More recent critical readings have explored the theatrical dimension. Richard Fly, in *Shakespeare's Mediated World* (1976), sees the play's striving against the theatrical medium as a strength, not a weakness; Susan Snyder, in *The Comic Matrix of Shakespeare's Tragedies* (1979), shows how it uses established conventions of genre to baffle audience expectation; and Michael Goldman, in *Acting and Action in Shakespearean Tragedy* (1985), relates Lear's experience to that of the actor who plays him. Maynard Mack's wide-ranging *King Lear in Our Time* (1965) includes discussions of the play's stage history and its debt to the morality play. It may be significant that the most thorough theatre-based study, Marvin Rosenberg's *The Masks of King Lear* (1972), which gives a scene-by-scene account of what actors have done, stresses the play's contradictions and presents a generally dark reading. As my own discussion will try to show, if we attend to the theatrical life of the play, we find it a series of dismaying shocks. This does not mean that 'Christian' or 'affirmative' readings are necessarily put out of court, but it does mean that they are constantly being tested by challenges from within the text, challenges which come to a large extent through theatrical means.

·1·

The Dramatic Idiom

To begin at the ending: in his 1765 edition of Shakespeare, Samuel Johnson confessed, 'I was many years ago so shocked by *Cordelia*'s death, that I know not whether I ever endured to read again the last scenes of the play till I undertook to revise them as an editor'. For Johnson the shock was not just emotional; it was a violation of expectation at several levels: '*Shakespeare* has suffered the virtue of *Cordelia* to perish in a just cause, contrary to the natural ideas of justice, the hope of the reader, and, what is yet more strange, to the faith of the chronicles'.[1] Gāmini Salgādo adds to Johnson's sense of baffled expectation the idea that tragedy itself has been violated: 'the death of Cordelia subverts almost all our expectations of tragedy. It robs the hero of tragic illumination and his suffering of 'educative' or redemptive power . . . it makes it impossible for the survivors to give a convincing and true account of the tragic hero's achievement'.[2] Cordelia's death, then, is not just a painful shock but an event that baffles our attempts to understand it, or to gain something from it. There is perhaps no play of Shakespeare's that so hinges on one moment as *King Lear* hinges on the death of Cordelia; and it is a moment that seems to resist interpretation. Dr Johnson has not been the only one to turn away from it, though his statement is more honest and forthright than most. I once

1

asked a group of students in an examination to write about
justice in King Lear. I was struck by the number who tried to
construct a neat moral scheme for the play, in which the
good were rewarded and the wicked punished, and who
dealt with the death of Cordelia by the simple expedient of
not mentioning it at all. This could hardly have been
inattention or forgetfulness: they were declaring by silence
that they could not cope with it.

But if this death violates the expectations we bring to the
play, does it violate the play itself? We may be tempted to
think so. The action of Othello leads inexorably to the death
of Desdemona, and from the beginning of the last scene
onwards our attention is focused on that figure on the bed.
Shakespeare seems to have taken equal pains in the last
scene of King Lear to take our attention away from Lear and
Cordelia. The old king and his daughter are marched off to
prison and the stage is given over to the squabbles of the
victors, the combat between Edgar and Edmond, the deaths
of Goneril and Regan—a busy and rather fussy action that
distracts us to the point where, as a reference to Lear and
Cordelia prompts Albany to exclaim, 'Great thing of us
forgot!' (V.iii. 211), we realize we have forgotten too.[3]
According to A. C. Bradley, 'this catastrophe, unlike those
of all the other mature tragedies, does not seem at all
inevitable. It is not even satisfactorily motived. In fact it
seems expressly designed to fall suddenly like a bolt from a
sky cleared by the vanished storm'.[4]

Bradley is referring to the impression we get from much
of the last scene that the right has prevailed. Albany is
asserting himself; Edgar defeats Edmond in a trial by
combat; Goneril and Regan die. Nor is it the last scene alone
that creates this effect. From the blinding of Gloucester
onward, the forces of good, helplessly in retreat in the first
half of the play, begin to consolidate and fight back. As
Cornwall puts out Gloucester's second eye, he is already
dying, stabbed by a nameless servant who has not only
expressed the revulsion the audience feels but acted on it.

Cornwall's death is followed in short order by the meeting of Edgar and Gloucester, Albany's open revolt against Goneril, and the return of Cordelia. Small details contribute to the feeling of restoration: Lear has lost his hundred knights, but Cordelia sends exactly that number in search of him: 'A century send forth' (IV.iii. 6 [IV.iv]). Even the military defeat of Lear and Cordelia is not a total setback. We know that in Albany they have a powerful ally in the enemy's camp. Moreover, the winners do not sound like winners. Success only exacerbates the tensions among them, as they squabble over Edmond's position, a squabble whose tone gets increasingly childish as we watch the fruits of victory turn to ashes. Regan is already dying, poisoned by her sister, who will shortly kill herself. Edmond, the centre of the dispute, has only a few minutes to live. Of the winners, only Albany will be left standing at the end of the play.

In a more pervasive and subtle way, the play's closeness to comedy triggers expectations of an ordered ending, with the defeat of the wicked and the restoration of the good. Every one of Shakespeare's tragedies makes some use of laughter, though the laughter can be grim; but none makes such pervasive use of the fundamental structures of comedy, particularly comedy as Shakespeare practised it. Lear's wilderness journey seems to parody the forest scenes of A Midsummer Night's Dream and (especially) As You Like It, leading Maynard Mack to call the play 'the greatest anti-pastoral ever penned'.[5] Stephen Booth has noted King Lear's many similarities to Love's Labour's Lost, both plays beginning with a violated ceremony and ending with a surprising death.[6] In King Lear, as in so many of the comedies, there is a full and significant use of disguise; the other tragedies hardly use this device at all. It is as though Shakespeare is employing the conventions of comedy and romance to set up expectations that he means to frustrate, leading us to expect the happy ending that usually goes with such conventions. Susan Snyder, in her very full discussion of this question, points out that 'for *Lear* alone among the tragedies, Shakespeare worked from a comedic source'. The anonymous play *King Leir*, published in 1605 but probably written somewhat earlier, is 'history . . . cast in the mold of comedy-romance'.[7] Leir and Cordella win the war and survive to a happy future; the wicked daughters and their husbands are put to flight, but do not die. This was the ending Shakespeare's audiences would have known in the theatre before his play appeared.

And this was the ending theatre audiences knew for many generations afterwards. In 1681 Nahum Tate produced an adaptation in which the old romantic ending is restored and elaborated. Lear, Kent and Gloucester retire, on Lear's suggestion, to a life of contemplation:

> Thou, *Kent*, and I, retir'd to some cool Cell
> Will gently pass our short reserves of Time
> In calm Reflections on our Fortunes past,
> Cheer'd with Relation of the prosperous Reign
> Of this celestial Pair

The celestial pair are Edgar and Cordelia, whose marriage is for the modern reader one of Tate's more startling inventions. Edgar draws the moral:

> Thy bright Example shall convince the World
> (Whatever Storms of Fortune are decreed)
> That Truth and Virtue shall at last succeed.[8]

This is hardly the point of Shakespeare's play. But it is a perfectly legitimate ending for Tate, who has really produced a new play of his own, quarried from Shakespeare. His play stood the test of time: Shakespeare's was not restored to the theatre until well into the nineteenth century. Moralising and sentimental, Tate's *King Lear* is not ours, but it makes perfect sense on its own terms. David Garrick was moving in it, and an acted reading of the last

scene I once saw given by members of the Royal
Shakespeare Company was unexpectedly touching. Nor is
moralising sentimentality the only alternative to the ending
that Dr Johnson and others could not face. In our time,
Edward Bond's *Lear* (produced 1971; published 1972 by
Methuen, London)—an independent play, but one whose
full effect depends on a knowledge of *King Lear*—presents a
vision of human society more violent even than
Shakespeare's, but turns toward optimism at the end. This
time the optimism lies in political action. (There is, by the
way, a similar optimism in Tate—not content with passive
suffering, the blinded Gloucester foments a peasant revolt
against the new regime.) Bond's key image is the wall Lear
has built, ostensibly to protect his people from their
enemies. All the resources of Lear's kingdom are thrown
into building the wall; it becomes an instrument and symbol
of oppression. At the end, Lear, a blinded political refugee
who has learnt from his sufferings, takes a spade to the wall
and starts tearing it down. He has hardly begun to work
when he is shot dead, but his action is not futile. As the firing
party leaves the stage, one of them looks back. Lear's
example is to be held in mind by those, on the stage and in
the audience, whose task it is to build a better world. On the
face of it, it may seem absurd to compare Bond with Tate;
but they both end their plays with a 'bright example', while
Shakespeare ends with a dark one.

Both before and after Shakespeare, then, there are other
versions of the Lear story; and they all turn away, as
Johnson did, from Shakespeare's ending. Even in the
criticism of Shakespeare's play there are attempts at
consolation which amount to adapting the text. The most
famous and striking is A. C. Bradley's decision that when
Lear cries, 'Look, her lips./Look there, look there' (V.iii.
286–7), what he sees, or thinks he sees, is returning life, and
he dies in 'an unbearable *joy*'.[9] It may seem unfair to call this
an adaptation, but Bradley has made a decision on a matter
that the text leaves enigmatic. It is a decision a performer

could make; but it is certainly not a decision he is compelled to make. Bradley's lead has been followed by other critics, such as Irving Ribner, for whom Lear dies 'in a moment of insupportable ecstacy'.[10]

The story of the reception of *King Lear*, then, is in part the story of a search for consolation in the face of an unbearable ending.[11] Whether the consolation is sought by changing the text or by seeking the most optimistic reading of it, there is an underlying feeling that in the play as written, Shakespeare has not played fair. He has taken the ending he found in his sources, the ending we want, the ending the play itself wants, and he has changed it. But has he really? Let us look at Dr Johnson's claim that Shakespeare has departed from 'the faith of the chronicles'. This is actually a half-truth. The play *King Leir* has a happy ending, and stops there, as plays can do. But history always goes on. The story of Lear and his three daughters comes from the legendary pre-Conquest 'history' of Britain recorded by Geoffrey of Monmouth. Shakespeare could have found it in a number of contemporary sources, including *The Mirror for Magistrates*, Holinshed's *History of England* and Spenser's *The Faerie Queene*.[12] There, it is true, Lear and Cordelia prevail over their enemies and Lear enjoys a few years of happiness with his good daughter before his death. So far, Johnson is right. But after Lear's death Cordelia's nephews rise against her (Shakespeare's Goneril and Regan are childless); they overthrow and imprison her. She kills herself in prison: in Geoffrey of Monmouth, for chagrin at losing her kingdom (p. 316); in Holinshed, for grief at losing her liberty (p. 319). In *The Mirror for Magistrates*, she stabs herself after an encounter with the allegorical figure of Despair. But it is Spenser in *The Faerie Queene* who gives her the death that Shakespeare will adapt: 'wearie of that wretched life, her selfe she hong' (II.x. 32). In the chivalric world of Spenser's poem, hanging is always a squalid and embarrassing death, and this is the death Shakespeare chooses for Cordelia. The crucial difference is that she is killed; she has not despaired, she has not committed suicide. We could say that it is the author of *King Leir* who has changed the chronicle story, stopping short of Cordelia's tragedy and so creating, by omission, a comic ending at odds with his sources. Shakespeare has not so much changed the chronicle as compressed it, accepting and intensifying its vision of a world without happy endings. This makes Lear's fate far worse; but—surprising though the statement may seem— Cordelia's is in a way more merciful.

The death of Cordelia, then, is not Shakespeare's invention but was always latent in the source material. And there are clues that it was always latent in the play. In the Folio version of the ending of Act 3 Scene 6 Kent alone, with no assistance from the Fool, carries off his sleeping master. The image anticipates the more terrible image of Lear carrying on the dead Cordelia. More important is the way the last scene circles back to the first. Just before Lear's last entrance the bodies of Goneril and Regan are brought on stage, and Edmond is carried off. At the cost of some theatrical awkwardness, Shakespeare is creating a broken version of the stage picture of Act I Scene 1 with Lear surrounded by his family. (Edmond, so far as we can tell, remains on stage throughout Act I Scene 1, but after Lear's first entrance we cease to notice him, and he has become so vivid a character in the meantime that his absence at the end of the play is the only way to reproduce the effect of the beginning.) In the Folio, Kent's last entrance is sharply juxtaposed with the reappearance of Goneril and Regan (V.iii. 204–5); this strengthens our feeling that we are watching the opening stage-picture being reassembled. But there is a link more fundamental than the personnel (and possibly the blocking) of the scene. Once again Lear is asking Cordelia to speak; and once again she is silent.[13] Lear demands something Cordelia cannot give: in the first scene he cannot have her total love, in the last he cannot have her at all. This circling back is not Shakespeare's invariable practice in tragedy. The early scenes of *Hamlet* are dominated by the ghost of Hamlet's father, seeking revenge for his murder. But unlike other revenge ghosts he does not return to gloat at the end of the play; Hamlet himself does not even refer to his father as he kills Claudius. The dead king, powerful and ominous in the play's early scenes, is forgotten at the end. So are the witches who open *Macbeth* in such a striking fashion. So is Rome in *Coriolanus*, whose affairs dominate the first scene and are forgotten in the last, as the hero dies alone in a Volscian city. In these cases the play seems to break away from its beginnings. In *King Lear* the last scene completes, with terrible exactness, the action begun in the first.

The play's end is latent in its beginning, and the main clues to this are theatrical: the arrangement of characters on the stage, the voice of Lear breaking against the silence of Cordelia. If we attend to the story or the moral scheme we may find the ending frustrating, unjustified, unprepared. And it is right that we should do so, for Shakespeare has set out deliberately to shock us. But if we attend to the theatrical life of the play, the ending is a natural climax, one to which the whole play—not as a story or lesson but as a series of theatrical experiences—is moving. This raises the question of theatrical surprise. If a surprise is too clearly anticipated, it will not be a surprise at all; but if there is no preparation, it will simply leave the audience feeling cheated. We should feel that we didn't see it coming—but we should have. Two examples from the plays of Shakespeare's period will illustrate the point. The ending of Ben Jonson's comedy *Epicoene* (1609) hinges on the discovery that the title character, apparently a woman, is really a boy in disguise. Beaumont and Fletcher's tragicomedy *A King and No King* (c.1611) solves the problem of King Arbaces' incestuous love of his sister by revealing that all his life he has had a false identity; he is not the king, he is not Panthaea's brother, and the play can end happily after all. In neither case is the audience let in on the secret, though Beaumont and Fletcher drop a number of hints. Most readers or audiences coming to these plays for the first time are, I think, surprised. Yet looking back we realise that in each case the play's title gave us fair warning. We should have seen it coming.

Shakespeare's preparation is neither so limited nor so technical. It depends rather on the dramatic idiom he has established throughout the play, one that would make the Tate ending, as a way of completing Shakespeare's play, an intolerable cheat. We will return in due course to Cordelia's death and Lear's; it is now time to explore that dramatic idiom and to show how at that level—rather than on the level of story or moral vision—we are prepared for the end. *King Lear*, a play that for so long was regarded as unstageable, has proved its worth in the theatre often enough that its viability as a stage piece no longer needs to be defended. But we can go further, emphasising how *fundamentally* theatrical it is, how much of its essential thinking is done by means peculiar to the theatre. One of its principal devices has been labelled, by H. A. Hargreaves, 'visual contradiction'[14]—a clash between word and picture, what is said and what is seen. Albany cries 'The gods defend her!' (V.iii. 231) and Lear enters with the dead Cordelia. Against our feeling of shock we set our awareness that this is only the last and most terrible of many such moments in the play. Kent, in the stocks, reads a letter from Cordelia, anticipating a positive turn in the play's action. He concludes, 'Fortune, good night;/Smile once more; turn thy wheel' (II.ii. 163–4), and immediately Edgar enters, pursued, planning his disguise as a naked madman. The wheel continues to turn, but downwards. (Editors have spoiled this juxtaposition by marking Edgar's entrance with a scene break; but Kent remains on stage throughout, and the action should continue uninterrupted, as it does in the Folio and the Oxford text.) At the opening of Act 4, Edgar congratulates himself on having hit rock bottom, the point where there is nowhere to go but up:

> To be worse,
> The low'st and most dejected thing of fortune,
> Stands still in esperance, lives not in fear.
> The lamentable change is from the best;
> The worst returns to laughter. Welcome, then,
> Thou unsubstantial air that I embrace.
> The wretch that thou has blown unto the worst
> Owes nothing to thy blasts.
>> *Enter the Duke of Gloucester led by an Old Man.*
>>   But who comes here?
>>>   (IV.i. 2–9)

He is forced to conclude, 'Who is't can say "I am at the worst"?/I am worse than e'er I was' (IV.i. 25–6). Later, having demonstrated to Gloucester the mercy of the gods, Edgar concludes his lesson, 'Bear free and patient thoughts' (IV.v. 80[IV.vi]). Then Lear enters, mad and crowned with flowers; Edgar, and the audience, have to pick up and start all over again. The moments I have noted contribute to the blackness of the play's vision; but the effect can work the other way. In the storm sequence, and the later scene with Gloucester, Lear rails against the wickedness of mankind, summarising the human race in formulas like 'The usurer hangs the cozener' (IV.v. 159 [IV.vi]). It is powerful, compelling satire; only in Swift do we find anything to match it. Yet the stage picture reminds us that it is also reductive. As he denounces the wickedness of man, Lear is surrounded by signs of love and loyalty—the Fool, Kent, Gloucester, Edgar. He hardly seems to notice them. But we do, or should; by their mere presence these characters tell us that there is more to humanity than Lear's bitterness allows him to see.

On one occasion the stage itself is used for visual contradiction. Self-conscious reference to the fact that we are in a theatre watching a performance may seem an inherently comic device—as at the ending of Congreve's *The Way of the World*, when Witwoud turns his fellow characters into fellow actors by asking, 'What, are you all got together, like players at the end of the last act?' Shakespeare was always willing to use this device in tragedy, sometimes for comic purposes, sometimes for more subtle ones. The Gravedigger's remark that Hamlet's madness will not be noticed in England, for there the men are as mad as he, reminds us that we are in London watching a play, since the joke works properly only for an English audience. Cleopatra's reference to the squeaking boy actor who will play her in Rome reminds us of the (presumably) more accomplished boy actor who is playing her now. There is a moment of this kind in the Quarto version of *King Lear*, when Edgar enters at the mention of his name, and Edmund remarks, 'on's cue out he comes, like the catastrophe of the old comedy' (Q.ii. 129–30). But Shakespeare seems to have found this too easy and conventional a joke, for it is toned down in the Folio text. What remains is a more subtle and powerful use of the theatre itself to comment on the action. At Dover Cliff, Edgar creates through language a vivid impression of the cliff's height and the terrible fall Gloucester has had to the bottom of it. But the moment when Gloucester falls, sprawling on level ground, reminds us of something we knew but thought we should ignore: that he is not at Dover Cliff but on the flat stage of the Globe. One of the basic conventions of Shakespeare's theatre, the verbal scene-painting that encourages us to imagine what we cannot see (the moonlight in the Capulets' orchard, the dawn breaking over the battlements of Elsinore), is here brutally reversed. The verbal scene-painting is a mere cheat. And so, we may conclude, is the whole action of miraculous salvation that Edgar has contrived to demonstrate the mercy of the gods; it is a mere illusion, and proves nothing. This surprise, too, is prepared. At the opening of the scene Edgar tells his father, 'You do climb up it now. Look how we labour' and Gloucester replies, 'Methinks the ground is even' (IV.v. 2–3 [IV.vi]). Our sympathy for the conventions of Shakespeare's theatre leads us to assume that Edgar is

right and Gloucester is wrong;[15] then we learn that the blind
man saw the truth after all. This episode prepares us for the
moment later in the scene when Lear declares, 'When we are
born, we cry that we are come/To this great stage of fools'
(IV.v. 178–9 [IV.v]). With our awareness of the theatre
activated by Gloucester's fall, we are aware of the stage not
just as a conventional image of life but as a physical presence
before us. Yet what is jarred here is not our acceptance of
the illusion that is theatre but our acceptance of the illusion
that is life. Change places, and handy-dandy, which is the
world and which is the Globe? Our own 'real' lives may be as
illusory as the trick played on Gloucester, and on those
terms the invented action on the Globe stage has as strong a
claim to 'reality' as the life of the audience does. In the
process the full paradox of the theatre is restored: it is a
place of fakery, but its fakery is a way of intensifying and
clarifying truth. The stage picture that Edgar has devised
transcends his purpose. Thinking to demonstrate the mercy
of the gods, he demonstrates instead the pitilessness of life
as Gloucester, seeking the release of death, hurls himself
against the unyielding floor of the stage.

    King Lear, far from being 'too huge for the stage',[16] needs
the stage for its full effect, not just as any play needs the stage
but also for reasons peculiar to itself. Its most characteristic
language is concrete and physical. Feelings are, in the strict
sense, embodied. The tortured body is a recurring image:
Cordelia's fault, according to Lear, 'like an engine,
wrenched my frame of nature/From the fixed place' (I.iv.
247–8). The body can turn against itself, torture itself: 'Old
fond eyes,/Beweep this cause again I'll pluck ye out' (I.iv.
281–2); 'Is it not as this mouth should tear this hand/For
lifting food to't?' (III.iv. 15–16). When Lear wakes in
Cordelia's tent, it is pain that tells him the experience is real:
'I feel this pin prick' (IV.vi. 48 [IV.vii]). Many of the changes
in the Folio text are designed to make the language more
concrete. When Lear attempts to strip, imitating the naked
madman in whom he recognizes essential man, he cries, in

the Quarto, 'Come on, be true' (Q.xi. 99). This becomes in the Folio 'Come, unbutton here' (III.iv. 102). The Quarto version of Lear's question about Regan, 'Is there any cause in nature that makes this hardness?' (Q.xiii. 71–2) becomes in the Folio 'Is there any cause in nature that makes these hard-hearts?' (III.vi. 35–6). If these are revisions, their direction is clear. According to J.I.M. Stewart, 'The blinding of Gloucester represents a sort of crystallizing of this element of physical outrage which the imagery holds so massively in suspension throughout the play'.[17] What was only talked about is now seen. But even a reader can feel the physical horror of the scene in the language: 'Bind fast his corky arms'; 'Out, vile jelly!' (III.vii. 27, 81). In language and action this is an intensely physical play.

When the contracts and relationships of the social order break down, the violence that emerges is not, as in Akira Kurosawa's *Lear*-inspired film *Ran*, (1985), the spectacular violence of war. The battle in *Lear* is the most perfunctory battle in Shakespeare. Rather, we seem to be watching the playground violence of children: striking, tripping, kicking. Instead of the epic clash of armies, which Shakespeare's theatre could suggest by exciting hand-to-hand combat, we are watching the low, undignified essence of violence, the hard, angry striking of body against body. There is a concentration, too, on the lower body: the tripping of Oswald, the stocking of Kent and Cornwall's 'Upon these eyes of thine I'll set my foot' (III.vii. 66). (How do you use a foot to gouge out an eye? In Peter Brook's 1962 Royal Shakespeare Company production the answer was simple: Cornwall was wearing spurs.) In *Macbeth* the language of violence is moral and poetic; in *King Lear* it is physical. The connection between the physical and the theatrical, as it applies to this play, is admirably summarized in Michael Goldman's observation that in the writing of Lear's part Shakespeare uses something like the modern actor's technique of keeping emotion fresh by focusing on physical objects.[18] The object can be as small as you like—a button will do—provided it is concrete.

Theatrical experience is not only physical but immediate: we move from moment to moment, carried along by the inexorable pace of the performance, unable to turn back (as we can in a novel) to reread and reconsider. More to the point, the economy of theatre means that a playwright cannot, and probably should not, round out and complete his narrative the way a novelist can. We accept a certain compression as natural to the form. But the special theatricality of *King Lear* takes this compression to extremes: disconnections and omissions are not merely allowed but virtually flaunted. A. C. Bradley, used to a more realistic form of storytelling, compiled a list of the play's 'improbabilities'.[19] More recently, John Reibetanz has labelled its method 'anti-narrative'.[20] In the excitement of the middle scenes we may not pause to wonder what has happened to Lear's hundred knights, but when so important a character as the Fool disappears without a word of comment or explanation, we cannot help noticing. The actions of certain characters are at times inexplicable; far from being distracted from this, we actually watch them hiding motives from us. Why does Edgar not come out of his disguise? He tells us, aside, 'I cannot daub it further . . . . And yet I must' (IV.i. 52–3). Why must he? In this case we can guess, though we are never told directly, that the disguise is a necessary part of his plan to contrive experiences that will cure his father's despair—but a simple revelation of his true identity and his true feelings for his father might, one supposes, have done the job more directly. And what is Kent up to? Cordelia tells him, reasonably enough, 'These weeds are memories of those worser hours./I prithee put them off'. He replies,

> Pardon, dear madam.
> Yet to be known shortens my made intent.
> My boon I make it that you know me not
> Till time and I think meet.   (IV.vi. 7–11 [IV.vii])

His decision is as arbitrary, his language as opaque as Viola's in *Twelfth Night* when she asks for 'Such disguise as haply shall become/The form of my intent' (I.ii. 50–1). In each case we ask, 'What intent?' and get no answer. Edgar, we may think, has a devious streak. But what motives can the blunt Kent be concealing?

In Adrian Noble's 1982 production for the Royal Shakespeare Company the Fool's disappearance was explained: we saw the mad Lear stab him to death. Watching the scene, however, I found myself quoting a favourite Goon Show line, 'I don't wish to know that'. The director had smoothed out something Shakespeare left rough, and one realized how much of the play's effect depends on such roughness. To tidy it up is to turn it into a different kind of play. It is as though, by the sheer intensity of its vision, the play does violence to its own narrative line. The world it creates cannot be reduced to a story in which everything is explained; it is not so much a logical sequence of events as a series of colliding images. Nor do we always have the satisfaction of knowing which characters we side with, despite the apparent clarity of the cast's division into good and evil. Cordelia's initial, unsettling coldness and Edmond's attractiveness are matters to which we will return in the next chapter. But we may notice here that our satisfaction at watching Cordelia come to rescue her father is skewed by the fact that this is also a French invasion of England. This is played down in the Folio text, but it is not removed altogether. The most striking reference that survives is Cornwall's 'The army of France is landed' (III.vii. 2), which from one point of view turns the blinding of Gloucester into an act in defence of the realm: he is a spy, a traitor, in league with a foreign power. This is a national emergency, and all rules go by the board. For us, nothing excuses Cornwall. But I wonder if the play's first audience, for whom national paranoia came more naturally and the Gunpowder Plot was a fresh memory, might have been more capable than we are of seeing Cornwall's point of view.

For us the scene is hard to bear but easy to react to. In the fact of such cruelty, we know what we feel. Did its first audience, inured to public cruelty in the name of public safety, find it more of a challenge?

In short, if the death of Cordelia violates our expectations about the play's story, this is consistent with what has happened elsewhere: explanations denied, sympathies twisted, a general refusal to tidy up. Our narrative expectations are bound up with our moral expectations. The death of Cordelia is a moral outrage that makes us protest not at certain characters—we are now past caring about Goneril, Regan or Edmond—but at life itself. We recognize in this death the brutal unfairness, the absurdity, of the world we live in. This is perhaps the key element in Dr Johnson's unhappiness with the ending:

> A play in which the wicked prosper, and the virtuous miscarry, may doubtless be good, because it is a just representation of the common events of human life: but since all reasonable beings naturally love justice, I cannot easily be persuaded, that the observation of justice makes a play worse; or, that if other excellencies are equal, the audience will not always rise better pleased from the final triumph of persecuted virtue.[21]

The question Johnson raises is a fundamental one; it goes back to the principal defence of art in Sir Philip Sidney's *Apology for Poetry*: that the poet's prerogative, even his responsibility, is to create a world better than the world we live in. Johnson complains, in effect, that Shakespeare is simply giving us the world we know, the brazen world, not the golden one. On the face of it, this might seem for the modern reader the right thing for Shakespeare to do; yet the fact that we still feel something of Johnson's outrage suggests that even for us the expectation in his criticism and Sidney's—that art should be finer, clearer, better than reality—is still at some level alive.

The sheer scale of Johnson's objection reminds us that,
more overtly than any other play of Shakespeare's, *King
Lear* raises fundamental questions about the nature of man,
the gods (if any), human life itself. But it is a play, not a work
cf philosophy. Its moral and spiritual vision, no less than its
f cory, is not only embodied by theatrical means but
determined by them. As always in Shakespeare, there is a
close observation of detail in this play, social detail in
particular. We see the order of society breaking down, not
in large abstractions but in small things: the stocking of the
King's messenger, Gloucester's use of the mild word
'inform' when he takes a message from Lear to Cornwall.
(The King's reaction to this is anything but mild: absolute
monarchs do not 'inform'.) The outer world of the storm
scenes is not a bare space where the wind sweeps over an
empty plain; planning his disguise, Edgar evokes 'low
farms,/Poor pelting villages, sheep-cotes and mills' (II.ii.
180–1). Yet the play also approaches at times the abstract
idiom of the morality play, old-fashioned but still available
in Shakespeare's theatre. In this idiom, allegorical type-
figures of virtue and vice enact fundamental lessons about
human behaviour.[22] When G. Wilson Knight writes of this
play, 'we seem to be confronted, not with certain men and
women only, but with mankind. It is strange to find that we
have been watching little more than a dozen people',[23] he is
describing the methods of the morality play. So is Irving
Ribner when he claims that Edgar and Cordelia are not to be
seen as real people but as parts of a thematic design.[24] The
naturalness with which Shakespeare can move to
abstraction can be seen in Kent's rebuke to his master:

Think'st thou that duty shall have dread to speak
When power to flattery bows? To plainness honour's
        bound
When majesty falls to folly.

(I.i. 146–8)

The nouns could all be capitalised; they suggest, in quick outline, an allegorical drama acted out by type-figures: Duty, Majesty, Power. The naturalness of such abstractions in Shakespeare's idiom can be emphasised by a glance at a modern attempt to recover it, the ending of Eugene O'Neill's *The Great God Brown* (1925). The hero lies dead:

Captain   (*comes just into sight at left and speaks front without looking at them—gruffly*)   Well, what's his name?
Cybel   Man!
Captain   (*taking a grimy notebook and an inch-long pencil from his pocket*)   How d'yuh spell it?
             Curtain

This is what happens when a writer who at his best is one of the great playwrights of the modern era tries to move into large abstractions—strain, embarrassment and an awkward, joking apology. In the English-speaking theatre at least, such language is no longer part of our native idiom.

But the expectations of the morality play, no less than the expectations of romance narrative, are baffled in *King Lear*. *Everyman* (c.1495), the most famous though not the most characteristic of morality plays, is characteristic in one respect at least: it ends with a message:

This moral men may have in mind.
Ye hearers, take it of worth, old and young,
And forsake Pride, for he deceiveth you in the end;
And remember Beauty, Five Wits, Strength, and
       Discretion,
They all at the last do every man forsake,
Save his Good Deeds there doth he take.

The action of the play is fixed into a message that is clear and unchanging. What the play says at this point it has said consistently throughout, and will always say, no matter how often we read or see it. And so we can take the message home with us, knowing we can always use it. No such message is offered in *King Lear*. Shakespeare's use of abstraction is not fixed and assertive but dynamic and exploratory. We see this most clearly when Lear commands, 'Then let them anatomize Regan; see what breeds about her heart. Is there any cause in nature that makes these hard-hearts?' (III.vi 34–6). The question about Regan becomes a question about human nature. And it remains a question. The fact that the line occurs around the middle of the play suggests its place in a larger process: the more we watch what particular characters do, the more we are driven to ask large questions about humanity. According to John F. Danby, 'At the beginning of the play we are watching an old man and his awkward family. At the end all we can see is stricken Humanity holding murdered Nature in its arms'.[25] Whether or not we accept his reading of the last image, or agree that *all* we can see is abstraction, we may agree with his general view of how the play has opened out.

It is natural for it to do so, since it begins with the first of human relationships, that of parents and children, and links this with the social relations of prince and subject, relations that carry with them fundamental ideas of power and property. '*King Lear*', writes Jonathan Dollimore, 'is, above all, a play about power, property and inheritance'.[26] 'Above all' may be pitching it a bit high, but these are certainly key words, and they emphasise how deeply the play investigates the social contract. Uppermost in the persecution of Gloucester is its physical cruelty: but the relations of host and guest, patron and client, are also violated here. Cordelia tries to restore Lear not just as her father but as her king. When Cornwall says to Edmond, 'Natures of such deep trust we shall much need./You we first seize on' (II.i. 114–15) we see a man improvising a new social order based on personal loyalty as the old order, based on established offices, breaks down. As we watch the structures of family and state collapse, we return to the basic questions,

wondering as Lear does if man is after all not a sophisticated
social being but an animal with pretensions he cannot
sustain.

In a typical morality play such as Mankind (c.1465–70) the
hero's fall includes the adoption of a false identity, signalled
by his changing into garments that make him look
ridiculous. He recovers his true identity at the end by
recognising he is a child of God. Religion seeks the meaning
of man in something outside man, finding him to be
authentically himself only when he is part of a larger picture.
And so the questions about man in this play lead very
quickly to questions about nature, the stars, the gods.
Because these are questions asked not just by the play but by
the characters—and often answered by the characters, to
their own satisfaction if not to ours—the play presents not a
single theology but a series of conflicting theologies. Its
method, in other words, is dramatic. According to L. C.
Knights, 'By the beginning of the seventeeth century to
some minds Nature was ceasing to appear as a divinely
ordained order and was beginning to appear as an amoral
collection of forces'.[27] Edmond knows what he thinks of it:

> Thou, nature, art my goddess. To thy law
> My services are bound. Wherefore should I
> Stand in the plague of custom and permit
> The curiosity of nations to deprive me
> For that I am some twelve or fourteen moonshines
> Lag of a brother? Why 'bastard'? Wherefore 'base',
> When my dimensions are as well compact,
> My mind as generous, and my shape as true
> As honest madam's issue? Why brand they us
> With 'base', with 'baseness, bastardy—base, base',—
> Who in the lusty stealth of nature take
> More composition and fierce quality
> Than doth within a dull, stale, tired bed
> Go to th'creating a whole tribe of fops

Got 'tween a sleep and wake? Well, then,
Legitimate Edgar, I must have your land.

(I.ii. 1–16)

His nature is Darwin's: survival of the fittest. Against this
imperative the structures of society, and the irritating
language that goes with them, must give way. But even if
there is an ironic edge to his religious language, Edmond is
still thinking in religious terms. He is serving not just a
principle but a goddess. And he is serving a law. He asserts
more than his own individuality: while he is scornful of the
notion that he is rough and lecherous because of the stars
(I.ii. 124–30) he seems perfectly happy with the equally
irrational notion that because there was good sport at his
making he is bound to be more vital than if he were got in the
stale routine of marriage.

Edmond is of course invoking nature to justify his own
ambition and his own sense of himself. He does so smoothly
and without strain. There is a greater sense of effort when
Lear curses Goneril:

Hear, nature; hear, dear goddess, hear:
Suspend thy purpose if thou didst intend
To make this creature fruitful.
Into her womb convey sterility.
Dry up in her the organs of increase,
And from her derogate body never spring
A babe to honour her.

(I.iv. 254–60)

Lear knows he is asking nature to be unnatural, to change
her usual working in the service of his will. In his
unconsciously ironic 'dear', his own language fights him.
And while Edmond sees himself as following the rules, Lear
wants the rules broken for his sake. In this light the King is a
greater rebel than the bastard: Edmond follows nature, Lear
attempts to coerce her.

As there are no theophanies in this play we have no objective view of the gods against which to test the characters' theological imaginings. But we do, at certain points, glimpse a nature that the characters have not merely invented. The first such moment is the outbreak of the storm. Lear is threatening his daughters:

> No, you unnatural hags,
> I will have such revenges on you both
> That all the world shall—I will do such things—
> What they are, yet I know not; but they shall be
> The terrors of the earth. You think I'll weep.
> No, I'll not weep. I have full cause of weeping,
> > Storm and tempest
> But this heart shall break into a hundred thousand
> > flaws
> Or ere I'll weep. —O Fool, I shall go mad!
> > (II.ii. 452–9 [II.iv])

Throughout the scene, as his daughters join against him, Lear has called on the heavens for help, protection, and at last for patience. No answer comes. But when he invokes 'the terrors of the earth' there is a rumble of thunder, as though he has touched some hidden spring of disorder in the universe. This, despite the fact that his threats have sounded pathetically, even comically, futile. The most eloquent pleas for justice and mercy are met with silence. But in calling for horror Lear has at last asked for something his universe can provide.

We may set against this the natural setting evoked at Cordelia's return to England, in her reference to Lear crowned with 'all the idle weeds that grow/In our sustaining corn' and her command, 'Search every acre in the high-grown field' (IV.iii. 5–7 [IV.iv]). In Shakespeare, the season (if any) is what the scene requires; here the play's wintry atmosphere yields to the luxuriance of late summer. The connotations of 'sustaining' are picked up when Cordelia

asks her Gentleman (identified as 'Doctor' in the Quarto)
about the chances of Lear's cure, and he replies:

> There is means, madam.
> Our foster-nurse of nature is repose,
> The which he lacks. That to provoke in him
> Are many simples operative, whose power
> Will close the eye of anguish.
> *Cordelia*   All blest secrets,
> All you unpublished virtues of the earth,
> Spring with my tears, be aidant and
>   remediate
> In the good man's distress!

> (IV.iii. 11–18 [IV.iv])

Putting these passages together with the storm scene, we
recognise the doubleness of nature in its dealings with man:
destructive and terrifying on the one hand, beneficent on the
other. We also recognise that both aspects of nature are
objectively valid within the play; and yet this doubleness of
nature, though not simply imagined by the characters, also
reflects the doubleness of humanity. Lear refuses to weep,
Cordelia is eager to. Nature responds accordingly.

We know nothing of the stars in this play. But the
conflicting views we get from Gloucester and Edmond
embody, like the conflicting views of nature, the character
and values of the people themselves. Gloucester seems a
little defensive about his astrological determinism:

> These late eclipses in the sun and moon portend no good
> to us. Though the wisdom of nature can reason it thus
> and thus, yet nature finds itself scourged by the sequent
> effects. Love cools, friendship falls off, brothers divide; in
> cities, mutinies; in countries, discord; in palaces, treason;
> and the bond cracked 'twixt son and father. This villain of
> mine comes under the prediction: there's son against

father. The King falls from the bias of nature: there's
father against child.

(I.ii. 101–9)

These are the tones of a man who is used to meeting
disagreement on a matter of importance to him, and so
tends to lecture; there is also in his desire to blame the stars a
moral evasiveness appropriate to the Gloucester of the early
scenes. Edmond points it out as soon as his father has left
the stage:

> when we are sick in fortune—often the surfeits of our
> own behaviour—we make guilty of our disasters the sun,
> the moon, the stars, as if we were villains on necessity,
> fools by heavenly compulsion, knaves, thieves, and
> treachers by spherical predominance, drunkards, liars,
> and adulterers by an enforced obedience of planetary
> influence, and all that we are evil in by a divine thrusting
> on.

(I.ii. 117–24)

Of course, he has his own interest in the debate. As one who
plans to carve out his own place, he is as bound to defend
free will, even at the risk of sounding like a moralist, as his
lax father is bound to blame everything on the stars. In a
scene that he could háve used to place the action in a cosmic
frame of reference, Shakespeare has produced instead a sly
prose comedy of character.

When we turn to the gods, the first question is 'What
gods?'. They seem, like nature and the stars, to be images in
which the characters express their own hopes and fears. In
the opening scene Lear uses them, as he later uses nature, for
cursing; and his stance is once again countered by
Cordelia's: 'O you kind gods,/Cure this great breach in his
abused nature' (IV.vi. 12–13 [IV.vii]). Cordelia, however,
places her main hope in the power of nature and human
skill: 'Be governed by your knowledge, and proceed/ I'th'

sway of your own will' (IV.vi. 17–18 [IV.vii]). She invokes
the gods but she trusts the doctor. While nature has an
objective reality in the play, the gods are conspicuous by
their absence. As Goneril enters to join Regan, Lear prays:

> O heavens,
> If you do love old men, if your sweet sway
> Allow obedience, if you yourselves are old,
> Make it your cause! Send down and take my part.
> (II.ii. 362–5 [II.iv])

Nothing happens. And what happens at Albany's prayer for
Cordelia, 'The gods defend her!' (V.iii. 231) is worse than
nothing. Alan Sinfield has accused the gods of this play of
being 'truly and irreversibly insane',[28] but that may be giving
them too much credit for existence. Thunder is a traditional
sign of divinity in action; when Lear asks 'What is the cause
of thunder?' (III.iv. 145) the mere fact that the question is
put shows the old answer is no longer satisfying.[29] Madness
was also traditionally seen as a divine visitation; here it is a
purely human phenomenon.[30] The change from *King Leir* is
striking: there, God is almost comically obliging. On two
occasions Lear and his friend Perillus are saved from a
murderer, and their rescue is accompanied by a clap of
thunder. In the second passage there is no doubt of the
connection of cause and effect: '*It thunders. He [the murderer]
quakes, and lets fall the Dagger*' (xix. 1739). This is morally
responsible thunder. And there is no question here about
the power of prayer: Perillus asks,

> Lord, which didst help thy servants at their need
> Or now or never send us helpe with speed.
> O comfort, comfort! Yonder is a banquet
> (xxiv. 2166–8)

Just such a demonstration of the kindness of the gods, too
glib to be convincing, is constructed by Edgar in the Dover

Cliff scene, a variation on Gloucester and Edmond's disagreement about the stars. This time the son, instead of mocking the father behind his back, works to change his mind. The starting point is the theology Gloucester has devised to account for his misfortunes: 'As flies to wanton boys are we to th' gods;/They kill us for their sport' (IV.i. 37–8). As in his speech on the eclipses, he is shifting the blame away from humanity, but we listen to him with new respect. Edgar contrives his fall, and his miraculous survival, as a demonstration 'that the clearest gods, who make them honours/Of men's impossibilities, have preserved thee' (IV.v. 73–4 [IV.vi]). Though still longing for death, Gloucester appears to accept the demonstration: 'You ever gentle gods, take my breath from me' (IV.v. 215 [IV.vi]). We remain sceptical.

Yet the effect of the sequence is not just a cynical irony at Edgar's fakery. In Act 4 Scene 1 Gloucester, reintroduced (as he thinks) to the naked madman he encountered in the storm, turns from his pessimistic theology to a more positive one:

> Here, take this purse, thou whom the heavens' plagues
> Have humbled to all strokes. That I am wretched
> Makes thee the happier. Heavens deal so still.
> Let the superfluous and lust-dieted man
> That slaves your ordinance, that will not see
> Because he does not feel, feel your power quickly.
> So distribution should undo excess,
> And each man have enough. Dost thou know Dover?
>   (IV.i. 58–65)

The last half-line, apparently a *non-sequitur*, signals Gloucester's determination to leave the world. But he no longer thinks of that world as meaningless. He is prepared to see in the afflictions the gods visit on man not random cruelty but chastisement and correction, working (characteristically for the play) in physical terms. Man must be taught to *feel*. Gloucester himself has learnt pity from his own sufferings and practises the charity he preaches; we see him do it. His charity is more impressive in that he begins with a concrete action ('Here, take this purse') which then builds to an idea; Gloucester's view of divinely inspired charity is rooted in his own behaviour. We still do not know which view of the gods is closer to the truth, or indeed if there is any knowable truth about them. But we know something about Gloucester, and his prayer could be seen as his way of teaching the gods how to behave.

This also suggests a more sympathetic way of reading Edgar; what he demonstrates is not the kindness of the gods but his own kindness, in the physical help he offers his father, in his desire to bring him from despair. Even if he is wrong about the gods, and even if Gloucester would be better off dead, Edgar is acting out of a human sympathy we can still respect. And in a way he learns from his father, no less than his father learns from him. Gloucester describes Tom as one who has been humbled by the heavens' strokes. Edgar, introducing himself in a new character, calls himself:

A most poor man, made tame to fortune's blows,
Who by the art of known and feeling sorrows
Am pregnant to good pity. Give me your hand,
I'll lead you to some biding.
                                    (IV.v. 220–3 [IV.vi]).

What he says of himself is more important than what he says of the gods, and he goes on to demonstrate his pity by saving Gloucester's life not from an imaginary ordeal but from a real man who wants to kill him, doing in reality what he has only imagined the gods doing. In a simple, theatrical way Gloucester's blindness calls forth not only pity but what Maynard Mack has called 'relatedness, which is [man's] entry into humanity'.[31] Because Gloucester is blind, Edgar is always taking him by the hand. In their scenes together hands become as important as they are in *Paradise Lost*, and for a similar reason.

Any discussion of the gods in *King Lear* must confront the vexed question of the play's relation to Christianity. Though written within a culture that was at least nominally Christian, the play, unlike *King Leir*, imagines not only a pagan world but a world in which the gods are cruel, or silent, or non-existent. What survives of Christianity is the moral behaviour of people—charity, pity, forgiveness, sacrifice. No Christian God sanctions these values; they appear in the play, as L.C. Knight puts it, 'by an act of profound individual exploration: the play does not take them for granted'.[32] But there may be more to the presence of Christianity in the play than this. Fragments of the Christian version of history appear in the dialogue; they are suggestive rather than explicit, but that if anything gives them greater power, for they imply a latent pattern of which the characters themselves are not aware, a pattern working at a deeper level than the easy pieties of *King Leir*. Cordelia, according to one of her attendants, 'redeems nature from the general curse/Which twain have brought her to' (IV.v. 202–3 [IV.vi]), and the language suggests not Goneril and Regan but Adam and Eve. In the final combat of Edgar and Edmond, justice is done to the sound of trumpets; this suggests the Last Judgement.[33] More important, Cordelia, 'Most choice, forsakén; and most loved, despised' (I.i. 251), has Christ-associations: she comes back to England with the words, 'O dear father,/It is thy business that I go about' (IV.iii. 23–4 [IV.iv]), echoing Luke 2:49. The word 'hanged' is often used for Christ's death by crucifixion. The naked, tormented body of Poor Tom, nails stuck in his arms (II.ii. 179 [II.iii]), may also suggest the crucified Christ.

But these Christian images are there to raise expectations the play will not satisfy, and their effect is either incomplete or skewed. If the trial by combat suggests the Last Judgement it also recalls, by a dark irony, the first crime: a brother kills a brother. As in Lear's mad visions, crime and judgement are disconcertingly alike. Whatever Christ-associations surround Cordelia, their most important function is to emphasise the terrible difference between the two figures when Lear looks for signs of a resurrection that will never happen. In the last scene, Kent's question 'Is this the promised end?' (V.iii. 238) suggests Christian hope betrayed. This is not to say that a Christian reading of *King Lear* is put out of court. There is no place here for a naïve optimism about virtue rewarded, or for a simple trust in the benevolence of God. But Christianity can be tougher and darker than that: it knows, indeed insists, that the world is wicked and unfair; and it also insists that God is finally unfathomable.[34] It can imagine Christ himself crying from the cross, 'my God, my God, why hast thou forsaken me? (Matthew 27.46)—a cry that seems to reverberate through *King Lear*. We might add that Christianity's concentration on the physical—the Incarnation, the crucified body, the resurrected body, the Eucharist—links at a deep level with the intensely physical nature of the play, making it in that respect at least the work of a Christian imagination.

But though Christianity may acknowledge the pain of life, it also insists that life has meaning, even if we may not always discern the meaning; that is is not finally absurd. And it is the fear of absurdity that *King Lear* in its darkest moments explores. From Cordelia's first use of it—reiterated and emphasised in the Folio revision—the word 'nothing' reverberates through the play. When the Fool builds the image of the split egg into the accusation, 'Thou hast pared thy wit o' both sides and left nothing i'th' middle' (I.iv. 168–9), we touch on the very modern fear of the disappearance of identity, dramatised in Ibsen's *Peer Gynt* when Peer, looking for an image of his essential self, takes apart an onion and finds, like Lear, nothing in the middle. The fear that the world itself is meaningless is suggested in Gloucester's address to Lear, 'O ruined piece of nature! This great world/Shall we wear out to nought' (IV.v. 130–1 [IV.vi]). Instead of ending in a grand scene of judgement, the

world will simply run down and die, an exhausted organism.
In the religion, science and poetry of Shakespeare's time,
numbers were held to be deeply significant: there was a
whole science of numerology, reflecting the ultimate
ordering of the universe. Here, the reason why the seven
stars are no more than seven is simply 'Because they are not
eight' (I.v. 37).

Albany is one of those who tries to see a moral order in
the world. When he hears that Cornwall was killed in the act
of blinding Gloucester, he exclaims,

> This shows you are above,
> You justicers, that these our nether crimes
> So speedily can venge. But, O poor Gloucester!
> Lost he his other eye?
>
> (IV.ii. 46–9)

The justicers, we have to conclude, are not so efficient as
they might be. But if they were, how would we like it?
According to Robert Bechtold Heilman, the play has a
fundamental belief: 'there is a realm of eternal law and
justice, of enduring reality which demands the loyalty of
mortals, and through that loyalty they achieve their
humanity'.[35] How do law and justice appear in the play?
Even Albany says of the deaths of Goneril and Regan, 'This
judgement of the heavens, that makes us tremble,/ Touches
us not with pity' (V.iii. 206–7), and of the death of Edmond,
'That's but a trifle here' (V.iii. 271). The first judgement is
'terrible, almost unwelcome',[36] the second is greeted with a
shrug. This hardly sounds as though Albany is accepting
justice and through it achieving humanity. And for many of
us one of the most repulsive moments in the play is Edgar's
summary of his father's fate:

> The gods are just, and of our pleasant vices
> Make instruments to plague us.

The dark and vicious place where thee he got
Cost him his eyes.

Edmond agrees: 'Thou'st spoken right. 'Tis true./The wheel
is come full circle. I am here' (V.iii. 161–5). But the circling
of a wheel is a mechanical process, not a human one. And in
Edgar's 'dark and vicious place' we catch a disturbing echo
of Lear's discovery of the sulphurous pit in the female body.
Does Gloucester's casual sin really condone the torment he
has suffered? And are we really meant, for the sake of justice
and order, to recoil in disgust from the human body itself? If
this is order, we may conclude, give us absurdity.

Disturbing as Edgar's moral complacency may be, some
critics have gone even farther. I quote, with some
incredulity, from Irving Ribner: 'We are not to suppose that
the fate which overtakes Gloucester is mere retribution for
lechery, for his sin goes deeper than that. Gloucester
violates the laws of primogeniture'—in other words, his sin
consists in loving his two sons equally.[37] The real value of
this kind of 'justice' is best summed up by John D.
Rosenberg: 'Like Job's pharisaical comforters, those critics
who find "poetic justice" in King Lear are guilty of a morally
shocking reading of the play'.[38] The system of reward and
punishment that Dr Johnson asked for is in fact present in
the play, and in its own way it is more cruel and alarming
than mere random violence. It is smug and self-satisfied; it
dresses up suffering as punishment; it postulates a world
without pity; it is finally, deeply inhuman. Gloucester is its
principal victim, for his suffering is far more protracted than
the endings of Cornwall, Goneril, Regan and Edmond. By
making us watch his punishment Shakespeare—again,
theatrically—is making us question the rightness of
retribution, making us wish instead for openness, even
randomness in the scheme of things, if this is what justice
looks like. We ask, in other words, for a glimpse of a world
free of justice. And we get it—in the death of Cordelia.

As our belief in reward and punishment cannot survive

the sight of the blinded Gloucester, so our belief that
absurdity might be liberating cannot survive the sight of the
dead Cordelia. In both cases I have imagined a particular
disillusionment that may not take place, consciously at
least, in the mind of every reader or audience member.
(There is an essay to be written on the use of the word 'we' in
criticism.) But I think the general process I have described—
an idea tested against a staged image of reality, and
breaking—can be seen as a fundamental method, perhaps
the fundamental method, of the play. It is by this method
that the play's exploration of man is made dynamic and
theatrical. One crucial example will help us summarise the
effect. It is a scene much beloved by those who try to find
consolation in the play. In the middle of the storm sequence
Lear, for the first time in the play, asks to be left alone. And
for the first time he *is* alone. He utters a prayer, not to the
gods but to humanity:

> Poor naked wretches, wheresoe'er you are,
> That bide the pelting of this pitiless storm,
> How shall your houseless heads and unfed sides,
> Your looped and windowed raggedness, defend you
> From seasons such as these? O, I have ta'en
> Too little care of this. Take physic, pomp,
> Expose thyself to feel what wretches feel,
> That thou mayst shake the superflux to them
> And show the heavens more just.
>
>   (III.iv. 28–36)

In the midst of all the fury there is a moment of stillness.
After three acts of wounded pride, Lear is learning pity and
humility. He is admitting, at last, that he has been wrong. He
sounds calm, rational, blissfully sane. We want to fix this
moment and hold it, as an achievement for Lear and for the
play. But the play will not let us. As Lear reaches his
conclusion, an actual poor naked wretch bursts on to the
stage, crying, 'Fathom and a half! Fathom and a half! Poor

Tom!' and the Fool cries, 'Come not in here, nuncle. Here's a spirit. Help me, help me!' (III.iv. 37–9). Lear has seen the naked wretches of the kingdom in the abstract, objects of pity, charity and understanding. But the first reaction to Poor Tom comes from the Fool, and the Fool is terrified. Tom is not just pathetically helpless; he is frightening and demonic. And when Lear sees Tom, his sanity, and his new insight, vanish in a moment. On the words, 'Did'st thou give all to thy two daughters,/And art thou come to this?' (III.iv. 46–7) he goes suddenly, clinically mad, losing touch with literal reality—and losing his selflessness as well, for his pity for Tom is all too obviously a projection of his pity for himself. In the prayer he was learning from his sufferings; now he is, once again, simply obsessed with them.

The surprise, like all the play's surprises, is prepared. As Harry Berger Jr has noted, Lear's prayer is curiously disconnected from the previous action of the play, which had little or nothing to do with his neglect of the poor.[39] As an achievement of insight it was always a bit shaky, and it collapses at the first blow. But what replaces it, the stage figure of Poor Tom, is not a fixed reality either. Lear sees him one way:

> Is man no more than this? Consider him well. Thou owest the worm no silk, the beast no hide, the sheep no wool, the cat no perfume. Ha, here's three on's are sophisticated; thou art the thing itself. Unaccommodated man is no more but such a poor, bare, forked animal as thou art.
>
> (II.iv. 96–101)

Helpless, vulnerable, and above all simple—Lear accepts Tom as an image of essential humanity, and does not judge him. Rather, he judges the others, including himself, for dressing up and pretending to be more than this. But Edgar has a different interpretation. For him the bare forked animal is a wicked animal. While Lear's voice is steady and deliberate, Edgar's moves with a quickening excitement of self-disgust. Tom has been

> A servingman, proud in heart and mind, that curled my hair, wore gloves in my cap, served the lust of my mistress' heart, and did the act of darkness with her; swore as many oaths as I spake words, and broke them in the sweet face of heaven; one that slept in the contriving of lust, and waked to do it. Wine loved I deeply, dice dearly, and in woman out-paramoured the Turk. False of heart, light of ear, bloody of hand; hog in sloth, fox in stealth, wolf in greediness, dog in madness, lion in prey.
>   (III.iv. 79–88)

Edgar moralises Tom as Lear does not. And as Edgar's persistent asides remind us, the figure who for Lear is 'the thing itself' is actually an invention, a deception. The paradox that Edgar has disguised himself by taking his clothes off suggests that to be naked is not, after all, man's natural condition. Nor is Tom really naked. As the Fool, with his usual eye for reality, points out, 'he reserved a blanket, else we had been all shamed' (III.iv. 61–2). Whether as a sign of Edgar's inhibitions, or as a concession to the actor's, Shakespeare has created a distance between Lear's speech about the naked man and the stage picture of Tom himself.

Where does this leave us with Poor Tom? Where we usually are in this play—in transition, unable to settle. The play is 'a process, in which all statements, however convincing when made, are liable to modification or even contradiction in what follows'.[40] To a degree unusual in Shakespeare, the stage represents not a fixed location but 'a place en route'.[41] The Folio revision, as Steven Urkowitz points out, emphasises 'concision, contrast and surprise'.[42] Passages that prepare us for what we are about to see are cut: the Gentleman's description of Lear in the storm (Q.viii. 3–16); the whole scene traditionally numbered Act 4 Scene

3, in which Kent and a Gentleman discuss Cordelia's return to England and prepare for her reappearance; Edgar's description in the last scene of his encounter with Kent, which prepares us for Kent's final entrance (Q.xxiv. 201–18). It is as though Shakespeare combed the text for moments when the action confirmed, rather than contradicted, the speeches preceding it, and cut those speeches whenever he could. Other cuts make for sharper transitions. At the end of Lear's reconciliation with Cordelia, we go straight from their exit, with its image of comfort and restoration, to the entry of Edmond, Regan and their army, without the coda that smooths this transition in the Quarto. A principal objection to the conflated text is that it loses the speed and momentum of the Quarto and Folio, the Folio in particular. We need these qualities if we are to feel as the play means us to feel— driven, disturbed, unable to settle. Having given the first word of this chapter to Dr Johnson, let us give him the last: 'The artful involutions of distinct interests, the striking opposition of contrary characters, the sudden changes of fortune, and the quick succession of events, fill the mind with a perpetual tumult of indignation, pity, and hope'.[43]

·2·

The Secondary Characters

To the audience, the experience of the play is one of shock, disruption, discontinuity. Trying to find our way through the experience, we may fix, as I did in some parts of the first chapter, on recurring ideas and images—suffering, justice, the gods. But readers have more time than audiences do to fit ideas and images together and find continuity that way. For an audience the main lines of continuity are provided by the actors. They are the medium for which Shakespeare wrote, and an audience's primary experience of the play will be through them. Sometimes the characters they play will be not individual personalities but units in a collective experience, as in the wooing scenes of *Love's Labour's Lost* or the final war sequence in *Macbeth* (Caithness, Menteith—who are these people?). In other plays, such as *As You Like It* and *Twelfth Night*, personalities will be sharply etched, and much of the play's dynamic will come from their contrast and interplay: Corin against Touchstone, Sir Toby against Sir Andrew. *King Lear* presents an amalgam of both methods. The characters are boldly outlined, sharply contrasted—yet so sharp are the contrasts that they move towards abstraction, with (for example) Regan as hard-heartedness, Poor Tom as unaccommodated man. But not altogether, for the presence of the actors will always anchor the characters in particular human reality. Even the figures of a morality play, faceless on the page, are never quite faceless in performance. This individualizing is essential to *King Lear*; if the characters were abstractions they would be fixed and meaningful, and we could count on them. Paradoxically, the more individual a character seems the more elusive and (in a sense) unreal he becomes. Peer Gynt, all through Ibsen's play, is obsessed with being 'himself'; the final image of that self is the onion that falls apart into layer after layer, and has no centre. So when Lear asks, 'Who is it that can tell me who I am?' the Fool replies, 'Lear's shadow.' (I.iv. 212–13). The initial meaning is that Lear, having given away his power, is only a shadow of himself; but to say that implies that his essential reality depended not on himself but on his attributes, and his surrender of one of his key attributes, power, has revealed the emptiness of identity itself. He is not Lear; there is no Lear. He is a figure going through the motions of being Lear. This, not despite but because of the fact that he has been so insistent on himself: his commands, his needs, his sufferings. The sheer desperate insistence of his self-assertion betrays a fear that there is no self to assert. And it may be no accident that 'shadow' is the word Shakespeare uses elsewhere (notably in the last act of *A Midsummer Night's Dream*) to mean 'actor.' This is not Lear, this is an actor playing Lear. (Breaking the dramatic illusion is one of the Fool's prerogatives in Shakespeare's theatre.) In the experience of a particular audience it is Richard Burbage, John Gielgud, Paul Scofield, Peter Ustinov. But it is not the actor either, the man we would meet in the dressing-room. It is the actor being King Lear, using his voice, his body, his personality, in the service of another identity. In the paradoxical double reality of theatre the identities of part and actor extend and enrich each other—and cancel each other out. The actor is Lear's shadow; Lear is the actor's. As in the use of the stage floor in the Dover scene, one of the basic conditions of theatre, a condition we usually take for granted, comes sharply and disturbingly into focus as the medium itself embodies one of the play's key insights, the unfixed and contradictory nature of identity.

Our primary experience of a play is of following a set of characters through an action; but in *King Lear* our sense of who those characters are, what they stand for, and what their essential reality is, becomes increasingly disrupted as we watch them. 'Character analysis' is a critical method out of favour at present; it was abused by earlier generations of critics who constructed elaborate biographies to round out into full human lives the glimpses that are all the play offers. The current view in criticism is that Shakespeare's plays do not work like that: the troubles of the Lear family began not in the nursery but in Act I Scene i. There is a long-standing joke among theatre people about an actor who stops a rehearsal to ask 'What's my motivation?' to which the director replies, 'Your paycheque.' So much for character analysis. Yet we cannot deal with the question of character in *King Lear* simply by backing away from it. We have to move through it, from the initial impression of solidity and continuity to the dislocation and contradiction the play ultimately leads us to; and we have to remember that the experience of the play in the theatre is initially the experience of its characters. Peter Brook's 1962 Royal Shakespeare Company production is still discussed largely in terms of the director's vision; but my own memories of it—across a quarter of a century—are not just of its famous white walls and rattling thundersheets but of Irene Worth's smooth, insinuating Goneril, Alec McCowen's sharply intelligent Fool and Alan Webb's small, vulnerable Gloucester. Above all, I can still hear the grinding voice of Paul Scofield scratching new and indelible patterns into line after line. It is the characters, through the voices and personalities of the actors, who take us through the play. This chapter will examine the material those actors are given to work with. It is at this level that Shakespeare seems at first to be offering certainly, a clear-cut opposition of good and evil behind which we sense the conventions of the morality play, a division into black and white teams that means, as Maynard Mack points out, even such humble figures as Cornwall's servant and Gloucester's old tenant are 'impelled soon or late to take some sort of stand—to show, in Oswald's words, "what party I do follow" '.[1] This division is as sharp in King Lear as it is anywhere in Shakespeare; it is as though his fear that the universe is inscrutable and even absurd has made Shakespeare grasp at certainty in the sphere of human morality and human behaviour; or as though he felt that the extraordinary central figure needed a clear and simple supporting structure. The final chapter will consider Lear himself; but first I would like to examine the process by which the clear structure of good and evil characters breaks and dissolves, as the characters themselves become not only individualized but internally contradictory and unpredictable.

Let us begin with the black team, and with the distinction Shakespeare draws between evil as embodied in Goneril and Regan and evil as embodied in Edmond. Seen from a distance, Goneril and Regan are the wicked sisters of the Cinderella story. But Shakespeare gets much closer than that. What we hear when they are first alone on stage is not obvious, conniving villainy but the voice of common sense. The opening scene, having begun in prose with the easy gossip of Gloucester and Kent, descends to prose again:

Goneril   You see how full of changes his age is. The observation we have made of it hath been little. He always loved our sister most, and with what poor judgment he hath cast her off appears too grossly.

Regan   'Tis the infirmity of his age; yet he hath ever but slenderly known himself.

Goneril   The best and soundest of his time hath been but rash; then must we look from his age to receive not alone the imperfections of long-engrafted condition, but therewithal the

> unruly waywardness that infirm and choleric
> years bring with them.
>
> Regan   Such unconstant starts are we like to have from
> him as this of Kent's banishment.
>
> Goneril There is further compliment of leave-taking
> between France and him. Pray you, let us sit
> together. If our father carry authority with
> such disposition as he bears, this last surrender
> of his will but offend us.
>
> (I.i. 288–304)

Everything they say is either true or credible. The tone is flat
and neutral. Searching for some kind of emotional
colouring, we may imagine a flicker of contempt on
'compliment of leave-taking', an impatience with the
routines of courtesy; we may imagine an edge of resentment
or anxiety throughout. But there is no point where either
performer is compelled to show feeling. Most remarkably,
the statement that Lear always loved Cordelia best seems
quite without rancour; it is a fact to be added to the other
facts. Yet here the paradox of Goneril and Regan begins:
that they are *not* driven by sibling rivalry with Cordelia is
just the problem. If they cared about where Lear bestowed
his love that would show they cared about Lear, and about
love. They care about neither. Their only concern is their
own convenience. Not power or position, but simply
convenience. Lear is going to be a nuisance. Everything they
say is true and sensible: how many of us, faced with a senile
king and a hundred knights as house guests, would react
differently? Yet the passage is chilling because there is so
little in it. Jealousy, spite, eagerness for power, or revenge—
we might have expected any or all of these, and we get none
of them. Regan seems if anything more alarming than
Goneril, because she is even emptier. Goneril is the
executive, setting out such ideas as they have; Regan simply
echoes her. If Goneril's watchword is 'me', Regan's is 'me
too'.

When battle is first struck between Lear and Goneril, it is on the issue of convenience. There is a stage tradition, going back at least to Peter Brook's production, of showing Lear and his knights as a noisy, ill-mannered crew whose behaviour justifies Goneril's complaints. Critics debate the justice of this reading:[2] on the behaviour of the knights the text gives only the conflicting evidence of Goneril and Lear, neither of whom inspires confidence as a witness. But Lear himself, on his return from hunting, is rough and boisterous enough to suggest that any tidy housekeeper would find him an uncomfortable presence. Goneril's style is different. She produces a confrontation not by counterattack but by coldness and withdrawal:

> When he returns from hunting
> I will not speak with him. Say I am sick.
> If you come slack of former services
> You shall do well; the fault of it I'll answer.
> . . .
> Put on what weary negligence you please,
> You and your fellows. I'd have it come to question.
>
> (I.iii. 7–13)

Oswald follows orders: the confrontation in the next scene begins with his simply walking across the stage and saying nothing but 'So please you—' (I.iv. 45). The first blows are struck by Lear and Kent. When Goneril threatens action of her own, it is in negative, sideways language, so convoluted as to be almost incomprehensible:

> the fault
> Would not scape censure, nor the redresses sleep
> Which in the tender of a wholesome weal
> Might in their working do you that offence,
> Which else were shame, but then necessity
> Will call discreet proceeding.
>
> (I.iv. 191–6)

Necessity, discreet proceeding—the language is that of an
old-fashioned schoolmistress or a minor bureaucrat. The
Fool cuts through it to see animal savagery beneath:

> For, you know, nuncle,
> The hedge-sparrow fed the cuckoo so long
> That it's had it head bit off by its young
>
> (I.iv 197–9)

But such aggressive violence would in a way be more natural
than what we actually see: a cold assertion of decency and
order, yet so negative in its phrasing that 'assertion' seems
the wrong word.

Regan's ploy when drawn into the confrontation is to
leave home:

> Our father he hath writ, so hath our sister,
> Of differences which I at least thought fit
> To answer from our home.
>
> (II.i. 121–3)

She is an even cannier housekeeper than Goneril: if there is
to be any mess it will be on Gloucester's carpet, not hers.
They appear to be not attacking Lear but simply protecting
themselves: their tactics are to withdraw and deny. So far we
seem to be dealing with petty meanness, an evil—if it is
evil—that has no scale, no spiritual dimension, nothing like
Iago's 'divinity of hell'. But as Lear puts pressure on them, a
moral abyss begins to open:

>   Return with her?
> Persuade me rather to be slave and sumpter
> To this detested groom.
> Goneril   At your choice, sir.
> Lear
>   I prithee, daughter, do not make me mad.
>   (II.ii. 338–91 [II. iv])

Lear thought he was being ironic. Then he realises with a
shock of incredulity—and so do we—that she would do it.
There is a level missing in Goneril and Regan. According to
Edwin Muir, what they lack is memory: 'Having no
memory, they have no responsibility, and no need,
therefore, to treat their father differently from any other
troublesome old man'. He adds, 'they seem to come from
nowhere and to be on the way to nowhere; they have words
and acts only to meet the momentary emergency, the
momentary appetite; their speech is therefore strikingly
deficient in imagery, and consists of a sequence of pitiless
truisms'.[3] Muir's insight that there is something missing is
acute; but I wonder if it is memory. They remember their
father's past behaviour, and they look to their own future
convenience; there is at least that much temporal continuity
in their lives. I think what is missing might better be called
censorship. Most people have cruel or violent impulses but
are able to suppress them; we know there are certain things
we are not supposed to do. Goneril and Regan do not
appear to know this. When an old man is bound and
helpless in a chair, there is no reason not to pluck his beard,
no reason not to put out his eyes. (The first idea is Regan's,
the second Goneril's; Cornwall merely carries it out.) They
do not have to work themselves up to cruelty; it is there,
without effort. When Lear on his own initiative retreats into
the storm, there is no reason not to let him go. Goneril
remarks, ' 'Tis his own blame;/Hath put himself from rest,
and must needs taste his folly' (II.ii. 462–3 [II.iv]). Regan
adds that it might even be good for him:

> O Sir, to wilful men
> The injuries that they themselves procure
> Must be their schoolmasters.
>
> (II.ii. 474–6 [II.iv])

The criticism that holds Lear's sufferings to be justified as a learning experience finds support here. Or, as Granville-Barker exclaims, 'What moralists!'[4]

What begins as common sense opens out into a terrifying blankness, a moral idiocy. In Goneril and Regan we confront, to use a term coined to describe Nazi war criminals, the banality of evil. If this is a surprise it is, like the play's other surprises, prepared. Their speeches in the love-test appeared at first to be merely the ordinary flattery we might have expected. Here is Goneril's:

> Sir, I love you more than words can wield the matter;
> Dearer than eyesight, space, and liberty;
> Beyond what can be valued, rich or rare,
> No less than life; with grace, health, beauty, honour;
> As much as child e'er loved or father found;
> A love that makes breath poor and speech unable.
> Beyond all manner of so much I love you.

And here, Regan's:

> I am made of that self mettle as my sister,
> And prize me at her worth. In my true heart
> I find she names my very deed of love—
> Only she comes too short, that I profess
> Myself an enemy to all other joys
> Which the most precious square of sense possesses,
> And find I am alone felicitate
> In your dear highness' love.
>
> (I.i. 55–61, 69–76)

All Goneril does is measure the *quantity* of her love. All Regan does is offer more of the same. They make no attempt to *describe* their love, and we realise in retrospect that they cannot, because they have no idea what love might feel like. Their speeches are fundamentally stupid. A hypocrite should at least be able to give a passable imitation of the

virtue he pretends, but that requires some knowledge of it.
Goneril and Regan have none.

They may think of their later rivalry for Edmond as love.
He himself seems to think of it that way: 'Yet Edmond was
beloved' (V.iii. 215). But if this is seriously meant it is one of
his least perceptive remarks. The passion that drives them is
not desire for Edmond but jealousy of each other. From
early in the play we have seen a tension growing between
them, beginning with Regan's quiet insistence that Goneril
has the first turn at entertaining Lear (I.i. 286–7), and
Goneril's anxiety that they maintain a common front, a
point on which she does not altogether trust her sister: 'If
she sustain him and his hundred knights/When I have
showed th'unfitness–' (I.iv. 311–12). Regan seems
determined not so much that she should have Edmond as
that Goneril should not:

Regan	. . . Tell me but only—but then speak the truth— Do you not love my sister?
Edmond	In honoured love.
Regan	But have you never found my brother's way To the forfended place?
Edmond	No, by mine honour, madam.
Regan	I never shall endure her. Dear my lord, Be not familiar with her.

(V.i. 8-13)

In the Quarto this is followed moments later by Goneril's
aside on her entrance, 'I had rather lose the battle than that
sister/Should loosen him and me' (Q.xxii. 20–1). If
Shakespeare cut the line, it may be because we hardly need
it. Both sisters desire Edmond physically; but as they are
incapable of love, they are incapable of natural sexual

enjoyment, Gloucester's 'good sport'. Regan has a nasty obsession with the question of whether Edmond has got into Goneril's body. In the Quarto, he remarks, 'That thought abuses you' (Q. xxii. 12), and indeed we may suppose that Regan spends many of her waking hours imagining Goneril and Edmond in the act. The 'forfended place' is Lear's sulphurous pit, Edgar's dark and vicious place; but it lacks the imaginative dimension for her that it has for them. It is simply something forbidden, like a prohibition in a children's game. Goneril's desire for Edmond is a function not only of her jealousy of Regan but of her irritation at having to share a bed with Albany:

> O, the difference of man and man!
> To thee a woman's services are due;
> My fool usurps my body.
>
> (IV.ii. 27–9)

We come down, as so often in the play, to the physical; and at this level Goneril and Regan feel not pleasure or desire but irritation. What was missing in their first dialogue was any sense of motivated evil; when something like it appears in their rivalry for Edmond it is low, mean and not quite human.

It is revealing to compare Goneril and Regan with their equivalents in *King Leir*. In the earlier play Gonorill expresses an ordinary human motive:

> I marvel, *Ragan*, how you can indure
> To see that proud pert Peat, our youngest sister,
> So slightly to account of us, her elders,
> As if we were no better then her selfe!
>
> (ii. 97–100)

And Ragan, towards the end, expresses if not guilt at least a fear of exposure:

I feele a hell of conscience in my brest,
Tormenting me with horrour for my fact,
And makes me in an agony of doubt,
For feare the world should find my dealing out.
(xxv. 2357–60)

Shakespeare's Goneril and Regan are not created out of
such normal feelings but out of absence and withdrawal.

The evil of Cornwall (on whom we need not dwell long) is ⌐
not so much negative as simply weak. His achievements are
to put one old man in the stocks, and blind another once he
is safely tied up *and* held down by the servants. Despite
Lear's persistent questions he confesses to having put Kent
in the stocks only when Goneril has entered and all his allies
are on stage. He needs support. He gets the idea of blinding
Gloucester from Goneril, and he has to work himself up to
it, cautiously and defensively:

Though well we may not pass upon his life
Without the form of justice, yet our power
Shall do a curtsy to our wrath, which men
May blame but not control.
(III.vii. 23–7)

The more Cornwall parades his strength the more we sense
his underlying weakness.

So far, Shakespeare's depiction of evil follows essentially
Christian lines: it is absence, nullity, a negative reaction
against good. And Shakespeare achieves something that is
not always achieved in conventional Christian art—there is
not the remotest chance that we will find this evil attractive.
Edmond is another matter. Not only does his story run
parallel to that of Regan and Goneril, but if we are tempted
into moral complacency by our firm rejection of them,
Edmond disturbs that complacency. We can see Goneril
and Regan's point of view only in a limited way, in our
willingness to agree that Lear must be a nuisance about the

house. Edmond catches our sympathy at a deeper level. In
the opening of Act 1 Scene 1 he endures one of the most
familiar ordeals of childhood: Gloucester and Kent talk
about him in the third person as though he were not there.
(Juliet has a similar problem with her family.) We are told
that Lear always loved Cordelia best; and we are told that
Gloucester loves his sons equally. The difference is that we
have a fuller sense of the nature of Gloucester's love for
Edmond. It is a rough, unthinking playfulness, well-
intentioned but galling. In his first soliloquy Edmond picks
away at the words 'base' and 'bastard' like a child who
cannot keep his hands off a sore.

He reacts to the injury of his birth in a way we can
understand: by getting back, asserting himself. Unlike
Goneril and Regan he has, from the beginning, positive
desires: 'Well then,/Legitimate Edgar, I must have your
land' (I.ii. 15–16). He has also something they totally lack: a
sense of irony. His flippant prayer, 'Now gods, stand up for
bastards!' (I.ii. 22) depends for its effect on his awareness,
and ours, of its unorthodoxy. Quite simply, he knows he
shouldn't talk like this; that's why he does it. His
recognition of an opposed scheme of values, and his
willingness to pay it the backhanded compliment of irony,
show in him a moral awareness that Goneril and Regan lack.
Though he has the dangerous attraction of a jungle cat, his
appeal is not simply at an animal level. The surprise he holds
for us at the end of the play, when he attempts to reprieve
Lear and Cordelia, is complementary to the surprise we get
from Goneril and Regan. As their self-protective common
sense turns to astonishing cruelty, so his predatory
selfishness turns in the end to magnanimity. A more
conventional playwright would have shown Edmond as a
repentant convert. Shakespeare is subtler than that:
Edmond's virtue is of a piece with his evil. The position he
aspires to involves not just property but style, and it is one
of the play's more acute social observations that the parvenu
takes greater care to behave like a gentleman than do the

established aristocrats, who never think twice about such matters. We see this most of all in the last scene, in Edmond's reaction to Edgar's challenge:[5]

> In wisdom I should ask thy name,
> But since thy outside looks so fair and warlike,
> And that thy tongue some say of breeding breathes,
> What safe and nicely I might well demand
> By rule of knighthood I disdain and spurn.
>
> (V.iii. 132–6)

This is a key virtue of the Renaissance courtier as described by Castiglione—*sprezzatura*, nonchalance—though in this case it is paraded a bit too self-conciously to be the real thing. Edmond shows a greater mastery of the gentlemanly style in the sporting flourish with which he takes his death:

> But what art thou,
> That hast this fortune on me? If thou'rt noble,
> I do forgive thee.
>
> (V.iii. 155–7)

Forgiveness here is not a religious or even a moral value but a matter of courtesy between gentlemen.

A. C. Bradley calls Edmond 'an adventurer, with no more ill-will to anyone than good-will'.[6] If Goneril and Regan see no reason not to do evil, Edmond at times can see no reason not to do good. He is an accessory to the blinding of Gloucester, in that he betrays him to Cornwall. (In the subplot's source, Sidney's *Arcadia*, the equivalent character does the blinding himself.) But he sees no reason why Gloucester should go on suffering. Regan reports:

> Edmond, I think, is gone,
> In pity of his misery, to dispatch
> His 'nighted life, moreover to descry
> The strength o'th'enemy.
>
> (IV.iv. 11–14 [IV.v])

One suspects that she finds Edmond's second purpose more understandable than his first, but she mentions them, characteristically, in the same tone. Nothing more is made of Edmond's attempt at mercy killing, but we may note the irony in passing: as Gloucester's good son denies him the death he so desperately wants, his evil son tries to provide it. When he has to be cruel he is, like Cornwall, defensive about it. This is especially true of his decision to kill Lear and Cordelia:

> Come hither, captain. Hark.
> Take thou this note. Go follow them to prison.
> One step I have advanced thee; if thou dost
> As this instructs thee, thou dost make thy way
> To noble fortunes. Know thou this: that men
> Are as the time is. To be tender-minded
> Does not become a sword. Thy great employment
> Will not bear question. Either say thou'lt do it,
> Or thrive by other means.
>
> (V.iii. 26–34)

Edmond's nagging tone suggests that he is fighting not only a presumed reluctance in the captain but an actual reluctance in himself. In the Quarto his tension communicates to the capain, who becomes equally defensive: 'I cannot draw a cart,/Nor eat dried oats. If it be man's work, I'll do't' (Q.xxiv. 37–8). In the Folio this is cut back to a simple 'I'll do't, my lord' (V.iii. 34), keeping the focus on Edmond's own problem. The last we hear of the captain's promotion, by the way, is Lear's 'I killed the slave that was a-hanging thee' (V.iii. 249).

Edmond's attempt to save Lear and Cordelia comes too late. His mercy, like his cruelty, needs to be worked up, and it simply takes too long. He announces it, moreover, with a sheepish apology that shows his sense of irony is still alive: 'Some good I mean to do,/Despite of mine own nature' (V.iii. 218–19). Is Edmond really acting out of character, doing something we had not thought him capable of? It may appear so. Yet the sporting magnanimity is consistent with what we have already seen. He has nothing to lose in practical terms—that game is over—and something to gain in terms of the self-respect we have seen growing in him all through the play. And so he behaves as a gentleman should. This is not just an unexpected twist at the end of his career of social climbing, but in a way the logical culmination of it. Through the figure of Edmond we are warned not to be too confident about dividing the characters into 'good' and 'bad'. There may even be a closer relationship between the brothers than we might at first think. Their names are almost confusingly similar. In a brief sequence in Act 5 Scene 1 each presents Albany with a paper to read (ll. 30–45); and this parallel action may be a theatrical signal to their kinship, something we see more clearly in the later moment when Edmond agrees with Edgar's moralising interpretation of their father's fate. It is not Edgar but Edmond who first introduces the naked madman: 'My cue is villainous melancholy, with a sigh like Tom o' Bedlam' (I.ii. 132–3), and his lying description of Edgar—

Here stood he in the dark, his sharp sword out,
Mumbling of wicked charms, conjuring the moon
To stand's auspicious mistress

(II.i. 37–9)

—has something of the demonic quality of Edgar's later impersonation. Each brother is a resourceful improviser, a shape-shifter, a deceiver. Opposed though they are, there is a mysterious rapport between them that works against the division of the cast into white and black teams, and that makes each character more open and dynamic than such a division would allow. Filtered through the medium of drama, embodied in the complexity of character, good and evil emerge as something other than absolutes about which we can generalise confidently.

As there are two brothers, there are two principal
servants: Kent's opposite number is Oswald. Kent says of
him, 'No contraries hold more antipathy/Than I and such a
knave' (II.ii. 86–7), and yet Kent's savage description of men
of Oswald's type, who

> Renege, affirm, and turn their halcyon beaks
> With every gall and vary of their masters,
> Knowing naught, like dogs, but following.
>
> (II.ii. 78-80)

could be a hostile description of himself. His salient quality
is loyalty; so is Oswald's. With his last breath Oswald asks
Edgar to deliver the letter he is carrying to Edmond, and
Edgar sums him up:

>   a serviceable villain,
> As duteous to the vices of thy mistress
> As badness would desire.
>
> (IV.v. 250–2 [IV.6])

Samuel Johnson, looking for moral clarity in the play, was
puzzled by Oswald: 'I know not well why *Shakespeare* gives
the Steward, who is a mere factor of wickedness, so much
fidelity'.[7] The reason may be that loyalty is morally neutral.
Kent's hostility to Oswald is the most naked and simple
hostility in the play; on their second meeting he beats him
not so much for what he has done as for what he is. Is this
because Kent recognises in him the dark side of his own
virtue? In any case, Shakespeare takes pains to bring the two
characters together, so that we will think not just about the
contrasts between them but about the similarities, ensuring
that our sympathy for Kent's loyalty will be neither easy nor
automatic.

Kent's outburst in the first scene is refreshing and
attractive. It makes a strong impression on the audience, but
none on Lear. His later, loyal service is of real value in the

storm sequence, but of dubious value elsewhere. His attack
on Oswald in Act 2 Scene 2 leads to a satisfying barrage of
insults, but does Lear's cause no particular good. As Bradley
puts it, 'One has not the heart to wish him any different, but
he illustrates the truth that to run one's head unselfishly
against a wall is not the best way to help one's friends'.[8] Kent
himself shows a rueful awareness of this, confessing to his
master that he attacked Oswald, 'Having more man than wit
about me' (II.ii. 218 [II.iv]). Increasingly, an air of futility
hangs over him. Shakespeare's arbitrary plotting is to some
degree responsible for this: in the later scenes Kent keeps
losing track of his master. Though he is a strong presence in
the first half of the play, his impact fades considerably
towards the end.[9] As he tells Cordelia, he wants little
enough for himself, 'To be acknowledged, madam, is
o'erpaid' (IV.vi. 4 [IV.vii]), but in the last scene he is denied
even that. His disguise is a romance device, and one of the
expectations behind this convention is that at the end Kent
will reveal his true identity and his loyal service will be, if
not rewarded, at least acknowledged. He gets this from
Cordelia; but when in the last scene he reveals himself to
Lear his old master's mind has collapsed, and the longed-for
recognition never comes: 'He knows not what he says, and
vain it is/That we present us to him' (V.iii. 269–70). In Kent
we see one of the most popular types of the Elizabethan
stage: the honest counsellor. Shakespeare saves him from
the woodenness that often afflicts such figures by giving him
a brusque, excitable manner that makes him distinctive. But
he also hedges his virtue about with reservations, and cuts
short his expected dramatic career.

   If Kent shrinks in the course of the play, Albany grows.
Our first impression is of a well-meaning man who is
bewildered and upset by the developing crisis but is not
likely to do anything about it: 'My lord, I am guiltless, as I
am ignorant/Of what hath moved you' (I.iv. 252–3); 'How
far your eyes may pierce I cannot tell./Striving to better, oft
we mar what's well' (I.iv. 324–5). Goneril sums him up

contemptuously: 'He'll not feel wrongs/Which tie him to an answer' (IV.ii. 13–14). But even as she says this, it is out of date. Albany's language is getting sharper. Oswald reports the change:

> Of Gloucester's treachery
> And of the loyal service of his son
> When I informed him, then he called me sot,
> And told me I had turned the wrong side out.
>
> (IV.ii. 6–9)

It is satisfying to watch Albany turn Oswald's moral inversions right side up. But though Albany lectures his allies, he continues to work with them; it takes Edgar to dispose of Edmond, and Goneril and Regan to dispose of each other. And the strong impression Albany makes as a moral spokesman in the Quarto and the conflated text is sharply reduced in the Folio.[10] His extended attack on Goneril, with its shrewd analysis of the origin of her evil—

> That nature which condemns it origin
> Cannot be bordered certain it itself.
> She that herself will sliver and disbranch
> From her material sap perforce must wither,
> And come to deadly use.
>
> (Q.xvi. 32–6)

—and its prophetic vision of the future—

> If that the heavens do not their visible spirits
> Send quickly down to tame these vile offences,
> It will come,
> Humanity must perforce prey on itself,
> Like monsters of the deep.
>
> (Q.xvi. 45–9)

—is reduced to a single insult, 'You are not worth the dust which the rude wind/Blows in your face', and a single generalisation, 'Proper deformity shows not in the fiend/So horrid as in woman' (IV.ii. 31–2, 36–7). Theatrically, the result is a quicker pace and a sharper attack. Albany is less discursive in the Folio, and his lines are therefore more stinging. But they do not show the full range of moral awareness we see in the Quarto. Perhaps Shakespeare came to feel that he had been too sanguine about Albany, giving the audience too easy a satisfaction; perhaps he wanted to cut back Albany's development in other to highlight the parallel development of courage and resistance in Gloucester. But in both versions Albany does develop. As we get less than what we expected from Kent, we get more than we expected from him. The common factor is that the figure of virtue does not have the rock-hard solidity of a figure of virtue in a morality play: he has the shifting, variable quality of life. We are prepared for this by a significant touch in the first scene, a scene in which the characters for the most part seem fixed in absolute positions. France exclaims of Cordelia, 'Gods, gods!' 'Tis strange that from their cold'st neglect/My love should kindle to inflamed respect' (I.i. 254–5). The insults Lear has heaped on Cordelia have had the effect opposite to his intentions: they have made Cordelia suddenly, unexpectedly, more attractive. France describes the growth of his love as spontaneous, and he himself finds it strange. It is certainly neither prudent nor sensible. But virtue, no less than evil, has its mysteries, and as it appears in people it is not fixed but dynamic.

The most complex figures on the side of good are the Fool, Edgar and Cordelia. The Fool himself has some of the quality Edwin Muir attributes to Goneril and Regan: he comes from nowhere and goes nowhere. His absence from the last two acts is notorious; but once we know the play we may find his absence from the first scene almost as striking. His repertoire includes a series of jokes about 'nothing', and

his own part begins and ends in absence. His song of the
wind and the rain is not all he shares with Feste in *Twelfth
Night*: when we first see Feste he is refusing to tell Maria
where he had been. Each fool brings a daylight sanity to his
play; but each has also a hidden, uncanny quality, as though
someone that sane is bound to seem a little strange. His
'prophecy' (an addition to the Folio text, one whose
authenticity is often questioned) takes him outside the
dramatic frame, even outside time and history: 'This
prophecy Merlin shall make; for I live before his time' (III.ii.
95–6). Riddles and paradoxes are his stock in trade, and this
makes him an acute critic of a world that has itself turned
upside down:

> I have used it, nuncle, e'er since thou madest thy
> daughters thy mothers; for when thou gavest them the
> rod and puttest down thine own breeches,
>   *[Sings]* Then they for sudden joy did weep,
>   And I sorrow sung,
>   That such a king should play bo-peep
>   And go the fools among.
>   (I.iv. 152–9)

He sees a reversal not just of social and family order but of
inner and outer natures. He, no less than Lear's daughters, is
expressing the opposite of what he feels. His rattling,
compulsive singing and joking convey an underlying
desperation: 'And I for sorrow sung'.

But there is another reversal that is more significant. The
thrust of his advice is nearly always practical. His first joke is
to offer Kent his coxcomb, calling him a fool for serving
Lear. But he also advises him to keep something hidden,
something in reserve: 'Have more than thou showest,/Speak
less than thou knowest' (I.iv. 117–18). He himself keeps
something in reserve, behind the pragmatic cynicism of his
advice:

Let go thy hold when a great wheel runs down a hill, lest it
break thy neck with following; but the great one that goes
upward, let him draw thee after. When a wise man gives
thee better counsel, give me mine again. I would have
none but knaves follow it, since a fool gives it.

[Sings]   That sir which serves and seeks for gain
      And follows but for form,
    Will pack when it begins to rain,
      And leave thee in the storm.

But I will tarry, the fool will stay,
    And let the wise man fly.
The knave turns fool that runs away,
    The fool no knave, pardie.

(II.ii. 245–58 [II.iv])

His 'wise' advice, to follow the way of the world, is the
wisdom of a fool. It is really folly. But it is a fool who says it
is folly—and so on: the paradox, in the way of paradoxes,
keeps turning over and over. What *is* fixed is the Fool's own
behaviour. For all his ironic advice about the wisdom of
time-serving, he will be the only attendant left to Lear in the
storm. (As in the 'Merlin' speech, he is prophetic: his
reference to the storm is our first intimation of it.) We see
here an effect that will be repeated with variations in the
figures of Edgar and Cordelia: the Fool's physical, theatrical
presence makes a statement at odds with his words.

The opposition continues in the storm itself. The Fool's
advice to Lear has so far been both practical and futile: he
should not have given his kingdom to his daughters. To the
question, what should Lear do now? he can only answer at
the same level: 'Good nuncle, in, ask thy daughters blessing'
(III.ii. 11–12). Later in the storm sequence we watch Lear's
mind going beyond the Fool's, entering a territory where the
Fool cannot follow:

Fool   Prithee, nuncle, tell me whether a madman
           be a gentleman or a yeoman.

Lear	A king, a king!
Fool	No, he's a yeoman that has a gentleman to his son; for he's a mad yeoman that sees his son a gentleman before him.
Lear	To have a thousand with red burning spits Come hissing in upon 'em! (III.vi. 9–16)

The Fool talks of madness, Lear exemplifies it. The Fool is thinking in realistic and social terms, Lear is veering into wild poetic vision. There may be no narrative preparation for the Fool's disappearance, but for Lear and for the play his usefulness is at an end. Like Albany, he has more to him than we thought, exemplifying a greater loyalty than he can make articulate; but like Kent he also has less, for he cannot adjust his thinking or his language to serve his master's real need. Kent remains, a faded presence; the Fool disappears. Yet his disappearance is not quite final, for it is impossible not to think of him when Lear, at the end, exclaims, 'And my poor fool is hanged' (V.iii. 281). In some way he has confused the Fool with Cordelia: both pragmatic truth-tellers, both unexpectedly loyal. A rapport between them is suggested early in the play: 'Since my young lady's going into France, sir, the fool hath much pined away' (I.iv. 71–2). Lear and the Fool toss the word 'nothing' back and forth between them, as Lear and Cordelia did (I.i. 85–90, I.iv. 129–33). Just as we had become so used to the Fool's annihilation that we had forgotten he was ever there, he returns, a shadowy image printed on the figure of the dead Cordelia. His words and his presence have been opposed, but his presence has been more eloquent. And it lingers unexpectedly after his words have faded.

If the Fool is elusive, Edgar is puzzling. He seems at first to be hardly a character at all, merely a blank space on which the figure of Poor Tom is drawn. Practically all we know of him is that he is on the run. When Regan asks, 'Was he not companion with the riotous knights/That tend upon my father?' Gloucester replies, 'I know not, madam' (II.i. 93–5), and a possible line of characterisation is blocked. (Even if Regan's words are more a statement than a question, it is not clear we should believe her, and in any case the riotousness of the knights is a matter in dispute.) Set against this line is the juxtaposition of Edgar's first entrance with Edmond's ironic reference to 'the maidenliest star in the firmament' (I.ii. 129–30). At the time, nothing is made of the connection, but it points more clearly than Regan's accusation does to the Edgar who develops later in the play. He speaks for decency and propriety, for conventional ⌐ morality, for patience and trust in the gods. He urges his father to 'Bear free and patient thoughts' (IV.v. 80 [IV.vi]) and when he finds him slipping back, cries, 'What, in ill thoughts again? Men must endure/Their going hence, even as their coming hither' (V.ii. 9–10). He tells the dying Lear, 'Look up, my lord', earning Kent's rebuke, 'Vex not his ghost. O, let him pass!' (V.iii. 288–9). There comes a point at which survival and endurance have to stop, and the optimistic Edgar is slower than Kent to see that Lear has reached that point.   ⌐

Yet this pious young man creates the figure of Poor Tom, who, as Gloucester puts it, 'made me think a man a worm' (IV.i. 34)—a lesson very different from the one Edgar tries to teach his father in the fourth act. Tom is not protected by the clearest gods but pursued by the foul fiend:

> Who gives anything to Poor Tom, who the foul fiend hath led through fire and through flame, through ford and whirlpool, o'er bog and quagmire; that hath laid knives under his pillow and halters in his pew, set ratsbane by his porridge, made him proud of heart to ride on a bay trotting-horse over four-inched bridges, to course his own shadow for a traitor.   (III.iv. 48–54)

The fiend, like a dark version of Christianity's God, leads Tom into sin and punishes him for it (though in Tom's mind the sequence is reversed as though to emphasise its

craziness). Men also persecute him: Tom is 'whipped from
tithing to tithing, and stocked, punished, and imprisoned'
(III.iv. 126–7). In the trial by combat Edgar will do justice on
Edmond; here, as in some of Lear's hallucinations, the
physical cruelty of justice is exposed. Tom protects himself
with broken fragments of the Ten Commandments: 'Take
heed o'th' foul fiend; obey thy parents; keep thy words'
justice; swear not; commit not with man's sworn spouse; set
not thy sweet heart on proud array. Tom's a-cold' (III.iv.
74–7). With childlike desperation Tom tries to imagine a
moral system in which there are rules to follow, rules that
will protect you. But it all comes down to the brute reality of
physical suffering: 'Tom's a-cold'.

That Edgar is not Tom, his persistent asides remind us. In
a typical effect of visual contradiction, the tormented body
he presents to our eyes works against the more sanguine
philosophy he expresses elsewhere. This time we get the
body first, the speeches later: as Edgar is taking his father
through despair to resignation, we remember what we saw
beneath the clothes he is now wearing. The physical
presence of the actor, together with occasional references to
Tom in the dialogue, make the link. As in the case of the
Fool, the character's presence and his words are at odds.
This leads us to speculate on the relation between Edgar and
Tom. For Stephen Booth, they are separate: 'Poor Tom . . .
seems more Edgar's fellow character than his persona'.[11] For
Harley Granville-Barker, ' "Poor Tom" is in effect an
embodiment of Lear's frenzy, the disguise no part of Edgar's
own development'.[12] Other critics have taken the harder
route of seeing Tom as indeed part of Edgar's
development—harder, because there is so little in the text to
go on. Paul A. Jorgensen's suggestion that Edgar 'wants to
find out what humanity means in a tough world'[13] seems to
fill in an area Shakespeare leaves blank, as does Lillian
Feder's claim that through his disguise Edgar has become
'conscious of the deceits that had been an accepted part of
his life at court'.[14] Both suggestions are consistent with the

Edgar we see in Act 4, but in claiming he is educating himself about society they may be looking in the wrong direction. For Lear, Tom is not a figure in society, but unaccommodated man, the thing itself. And he sees Tom not as self-educated but as self-tormented:

> Is it the fashion that discarded fathers
> Should have thus little mercy on their flesh?
> Judicious punishment: 'twas this flesh begot
> Those pelican daughters.
>
> (III.iv. 68–71)

The word 'pelican' triggers Tom's next line, 'Pillicock sat on Pillicock Hill' (III.iv. 72), where 'Pillicock' means 'penis'. In the last scene Edgar's reference to the justice the gods have done on his father, 'the dark and vicious place where thee he got/cost him his eyes' (V.iii. 163–4), conveys a savage disgust with sexuality. Of all the disguises Edgar could have adopted, he finds one that makes him torment his own body. Besides the pain of exposure, Bedlam beggars 'Strike in their numbed and mortifièd arms/Pins, wooden pricks, nails, sprigs of rosemary' (II.ii. 178–9 [II.iii.]). (Is there an echo of Tom when Lear tests his wakefulness in Cordelia's tent by stabbing himself with a pin?) Tom's fantasies are full of dark sexual imaginings: if Edmond thinks of married sex as a sleepy routine, Edgar, through Tom, imagines 'the act of darkness' as taking place on the edge of dream: 'one that slept in the contriving of lust, and waked to do it' (III.iv. 81, 83–84). In his insight that Tom is punishing his own flesh, Lear may have hit on a truth about Edgar. It is not that Edgar has any particular sin to punish himself for; for a chaste and moralising young man the natural feelings of the body are sin enough. And so he creates—and, as we have seen, moralises—the image of a naked madman pursued by demons.

Edgar's concern to demonstrate that the world is just, may have, then, a dark side, for justice involves punishment, and we all bear what from a moralist's point of view is the guilt of sexuality. Even his kindness to his father in keeping him alive, and making him *want* to live, may deserve the rebuke Kent aims at Edgar for his treatment of Lear:

> He hates him
> That would upon the rack of this tough world
> Stretch him out longer.
>
> (V.iii. 289–91)

Edgar shows no sign of hating his father; on the contrary. But there is unexpected, self-satisfied cruelty in his reference to the way the gods have punished Gloucester. Marvin Rosenberg claims Edgar is better at talking about comfort than at giving it.[15] While for some critics Edgar's ability to pick his way through a difficult world is admirable,[16] others regard it with some distaste. S.L. Goldberg finds Edgar's 'skill in the arts of psychic self-preservation . . . not much more engaging when practised on Gloucester's behalf than on his own'.[17] In the last scene there are signs that Edgar himself is having misgivings about his strategy of survival. There is a touch of self-contempt when he explains how he preserved his life:

> O, our lives' sweetness,
> That we the pain of death would hourly die
> Rather than die at once!
>
> (V.iii. 176–8)

Edgar's revelation of his true identity is what finally kills Gloucester; and in telling the story Edgar rebukes himself for prolonging the agony: 'Never—O fault!—revealed myself unto him/Until some half hour past' (V.iii. 184–5). The paradox of Gloucester's death—

> his flawed heart—
> Alack, too weak the conflict to support—
> 'Twixt two extremes of passion, joy and grief
> Burst smilingly.

(V.iii. 188–91)

—suggests other paradoxes. The brothers, whose unexpected affinity we have already noted, have worked together to destroy their father (even as one brother has killed another, who in turn has accepted his fate). Keeping him alive, the best Edgar could give his father was resignation; giving him joy, he gives him death, completing the process Edmond began. He now wonders if he shouldn't have done it sooner.

Edgar's virtues are real: loyalty, kindness, a sense of justice and a determination to make the best of life. But we catch glimpses of a dark side to these virtues: the sense of justice has an edge of cruelty, perhaps even of self-contempt; and the kindness is a way of prolonging suffering. Even the complexity and elusiveness of Edgar make their own point: it is hard to get a fix on the character, hard to be sure of our judgement of him. The sheer variety of his roles—since he is deceiving a blind man, all he has to do is change voices— makes him as much a chameleon as Richard III or Iago, and this is odd company to find him in. But Shakespeare may be suggesting that in the treacherous world of this play—which includes the instability of human nature itself—virtue can survive only by constant adaptation. And we may wonder how far it can adapt without betraying its own integrity.

Cordelia apparently makes a very different impression— simple, strong and clear. But she too is a developing character. As there are unexpected affinities between Edgar and Edmond, so Cordelia's development follows a line parallel to that of Goneril and Regan. Her 'nothing' in response to Lear's demand for a statement of love is in its own way as extravagant, as detached from reality, as her sisters' elaborate protestations. She too is exaggerating to

meet the demands of the occasion, though she sees those
demands differently. When she goes on to defend her reply,
we hear again the voice of common sense:

> Good my lord,
> You have begot me, bred me, loved me.
> I return those duties back as are right fit—
> Obey you, love you, and most honour you.
> Why have my sisters husbands if they say
> They love you all? Haply when I shall wed
> That lord whose hand must take my plight shall carry
> Half my love with him, half my care and duty.
>   (I.i. 95–102)

Bradley observes, 'There surely never was a more unhappy
speech'.[18] Far from countering Lear's absurd quantifying of
love, she appears to fall into it herself. Like him, she makes it
a matter of return for services rendered. Like the narrow
retributive justice Albany and Edgar see at work in the
universe, this kind of love is a closed circle. In Geoffrey of
Monmouth it is clear that Cordelia is testing her father, in
response to his test of her: 'understanding how easily he was
satisfied with the flattering Expressions of her Sisters, [she]
was desirous to make Tryal of his Affection after a different
manner' (p. 312). In Shakespeare, the effect is certainly to
test Lear, but it is not so clear that Cordelia has consciously
planned the test. We fall back on variations of Coleridge's
reading: 'Something of disgust at the ruthless hypocrisy of
her sisters, some little faulty admixture of pride and
sullenness'.[19]

Albany is one character who is notably altered between
the Quarto and Folio texts; Cordelia is another. In the first
scene her aside 'I am sure my love's/More richer than my
tongue' (Q.i. 72–3) becomes 'I am sure my love's/More
ponderous than my tongue' (I.i. 77–8). Lear calls her, in the
Quarto, 'Although the last, not least in our dear love' (Q.i.
78) and in the Folio, more simply, 'our last and least' (I.i. 83).

This toning down of the language associated with Cordelia leads to one of the Folio's most significant cuts: the whole of the scene traditionally numbered Act 4 Scene 3, in which a Gentleman describes her to Kent in language that many have found cloying:

> You have seen
> Sunshine and rain at once; her smiles and tears
> Were like, a better way. Those happy smilets
> That played on her ripe lip seemed not to know
> What guests were in her eyes, which parted thence
> As pearls from diamonds dropped.
>
> (Q.xvii. 18–23)

This leads to a quasi-religious climax: 'There she shook/The holy water from her heavenly eyes' (Q.xvii. 30–1). If the Folio text is Shakespeare's revision, he seems to have decided that this sort of decoration was not needed.[20] Instead, we go by a more direct route from the cold, limited statement of love in the first scene to something that transcends the mere lyricism of the Gentleman:

> *Lear* . . .
> If you have poison for me, I will drink it.
> I know you do not love me; for your sisters
> Have, as I do remember, done me wrong.
> You have some cause; they have not.
> *Cordelia* No cause, no cause.
>
> (IV.vi. 65–8 [IV.vii])

Her reply lies close to the 'nothing' of the first scene, and is almost as simply phrased. It is also, in its own way, as absurd and irrational as the cruelty into which Goneril and Regan have fallen. Cordelia has every cause. So has Desdemona, when she answers Emilia's question about who has killed her, 'Nobody, I myself. Farewell./Commend me to my kind lord' (V.ii. 133–4). But this is a saving absurdity. It breaks out of the closed circle of service and reward, crime and punishment. It denies a literal truth in order to state a deeper one: in love, there are no offences worth remembering. It cuts the chain of cause and effect that began in the first scene. If Goneril and Regan have remembered only that Lear is a nuisance, Cordelia has remembered only that Lear is her father.   Though her language is still simple, the Cordelia of Act 4 seems a richer, more extraordinary character than the plain-spoken but cold and prickly girl of the first scene. Yet that is not the last stage of her development. Once again, visual contradiction comes into play. As Edgar's naked, tortured body denies his pious and optimistic view of the world, so Cordelia's dead body is a sight that snatches away everything she has made Lear—and the audience—hope for. Her forgiveness of Lear is one kind of absurdity; her death is another and a darker one. Cradling her, talking to her, trying to hear her, trying to see her breath, Lear makes her even for the reader an eloquent physical presence. Her unresponding body is the last and most terrible of the play's images of goodness in the world.

It is also the last image of what happens to identity. Goneril's and Regan's bodies are dumped on stage and soon forgotten; Cordelia's is lovingly carried on, fondled, cared for. But it is equally dead. Sharply distinguished in the play, the sisters are finally alike. They come together, as Edgar and Edmond have started to do. And as the distinction between good and evil dissolves, so the logical chain of motive, behaviour and consequence breaks down. As Cordelia rises to the transcendent absurdity of 'No cause, no cause', Goneril and Regan sink to absurdity of a more squalid kind. They have, as Lear acknowledges, some cause; but no cause to go as far in evil as they do. In both cases the absurdity signals that something we might have thought of as human and normal—decency in one case, natural resentment in the other—is missing. So, theatrically, the play deals not just in presences but in absences: the disappearance of the Fool, the dwindling of Kent, and the long period when Cordelia is withdrawn from us, an effect reinforced in the Folio when Act 4 Scene 3, designed to compensate for her absence, is cut. Gloucester, Cornwall, Edmond, Goneril, Regan, Cordelia and finally Kent all go off stage to die. (Remarkably, the only characters besides Lear who die on stage are Cornwall's servant and Oswald— as though Shakespeare is trying to break the theatrical significance of the death scene, so often a way of giving a last defining flourish to a character, by giving it indiscriminately to a suffering king, a petty time-server, and a character who has flashed across our consciousness for less than a minute.) What gives Cordelia's body its terrible significance is the absence of Cordelia.

Often, when the characters assert themselves they do so through performances, making them seem detached from themselves, just as Lear becomes Lear's shadow. Edmond's almost animal need for territory leads him to an exercise in gentlemanly style, self-conscious and uncertain, and to what he wryly calls a betrayal of his own nature. Like an actor who has a fixed idea of his part he is reluctant to try something new, and the delay is fatal. That Edgar is a series of performances is the most striking thing about him. We can, I think, go farther than criticism has usually done in tracing a man behind the roles; but he is a man at odds with himself, fighting his own performances as he torments his own body. Like Kent, he is unable to stop acting and unable to say why. His words and his presence are, we have seen, at odds; there is a similar contradiction between the Fool's performance, his riddling pragmatism (a paradox in itself) and the plain unreasonable loyalty he expresses just by being there. The characters' words are an unreliable key to their natures; nor can they always manage the easier feat of analysing other characters. In the Folio, passages of articulate commentary, like Albany's attack on Goneril or the Gentleman's description of Cordelia, are cut back or eliminated. More typically, the characters greet each other's sufferings with brief, helpless words of pity that flicker, half-heard, around the edges of a scene. The realities about which the play is most articulate are the brute physical realities in the face of which all individuals are alike; Tom is cold, Gloucester is in pain, Cordelia is dead. In the torture chambers in which Shakespeare would find one of the more recognizable links between his time and ours, it is the body that is used to break the mind, to turn the articulate individual into someone who no longer knows what he thought he knew, believes what he thought he believed, or is what he thought he was. The world of the play is, as Kent calls it, a rack, and the lines of continuity we try to follow through the personalities of the central figures are like sinews that twist and break. The greatest and most contradictory of those personalities is Lear, to whom we should now turn.

·3·

Lear

One of the principal ways in which critics have sought consolation for the ending of *King Lear* is to note that, however much Lear has suffered, he has also learnt. Walter Stein puts it succinctly: 'The world remains what it was, a merciless, heart-breaking world. Lear is broken by it, but he has learned to love and be loved'.[1] Lear in the storm, according to Robert Bechtold Heilman, 'feels compassion, acknowledges his own failures, and lessens himself in terms of divine justice; like Gloucester, he has come to a new insight'.[2] The idea of Lear's progress is given a religious dimension by A. C. Bradley's suggestion that 'this poem' might be renamed '*The Redemption of King Lear*',[3] by G. Wilson Knight's description of the play as 'purgatorial'[4] and by Irving Ribner's reference to Lear's 'spiritual rebirth'.[5] Other critics have resisted this view. In the storm sequence, where Heilman finds growing wisdom, Jonathan Dollimore hears 'demented mumbling interspersed with brief insight'. Passages that for some critics are prophetic wisdom are for Dollimore 'incoherent ramblings'.[6] Combatting the view that Lear learns selfessness, Barbara Everett refers to his 'love of the "pride of life" that is involved in his first mistake, and that never leaves him up to his death. He fights passionately, at his noblest, against . . . the death of self'.[7] In her reading, Lear is not so much reformed or redeemed as intensified. This question is bound up with the question of whether Lear's experience is the full experience of the play. In the heath scenes in particular, according to L. C. Knights, the voices of the other characters are 'part of the tormented consciousness of Lear'.[8] For S. L. Goldberg, on the other hand, 'although [Lear] is at the centre of the play, neither his consciousness nor his experience comprehends all of its meaning'.[9] If Lear's experience is redemptive, and is the experience of the play, we can read the play as a whole through his redemption, and take a more hopeful view of it. But if Goldberg is right, we need to remain aware of the limitations of Lear's experience, and this will prevent us from seeing even his most positive insights as the play's ultimate statements.

Shakespeare has given us a point of reference to guide our reading of Lear, in the character of Gloucester. The use of a fully developed subplot is one of the features *King Lear* shares with Shakespeare's comedies, and one that separates it from his other tragedies. The parallels in the experience of the two old men are obvious enough: each misjudges his children, and is betrayed where he placed his trust; each is cast out, left to wander, and finally tended by the rejected child. But Gloucester always seems to operate at a different level. While Lear, in his first scene, is guilty of 'hideous rashness' (I.i. 151), Gloucester reminisces in a jocular way about an ordinary sexual lapse. Lear grandly divides a map; Gloucester is fooled by a letter. In the confrontation between Lear and his daughters, Lear storms and rages while Gloucester tries, ineffectually, to temporise: 'I would have all well betwixt you' (II.ii. 291 [II.iv]). Under pressure his resistance to evil grows, as does Albany's; but at first there is an unstable mixture of genuine, dangerous loyalty and ordinary time-serving: 'These injuries the King now bears will be revenged home. There is part of a power already footed. We must incline to the King. . . . If I die for't —as no less is threatened me—the King my old master must be relieved' (III.iii. 11–18). We can hear his resolution growing in that speech, from the cautious 'incline' to the final 'must'. When he is tied to a chair, and set upon by Cornwall and Regan, he tries to temporise at first, then throws away his caution and attacks his tormentors with exciting courage:

> Because I would not see thy cruel nails
> Pluck out his poor old eyes, nor thy fierce sister
> In his anointed flesh stick boarish fangs.
>   . . . But I shall see
> The wingèd vengeance overtake such children.
> (III.vii. 54–6, 63–4)

His own words give Cornwall his cue; Gloucester's reward for courage is to have his eyes plucked out. Even here, his experience is at a different level from Lear's. Both men suffer physical and mental torment, but the physical is uppermost in Gloucester's case, the mental in Lear's. Gloucester's mind is always clear, and once he is blind he sees a path ahead of him. For the rest of the play he seeks for death, a thought that never once enters the mind of Lear.

Gloucester himself clarifies, and moralises, his experience. In the first moments of his blindness he learns the truth about his two sons, and declares, 'O, my follies! Then Edgar was abused./Kind gods, forgive me that, and prosper him!' (III.vii. 89–90). He is unquestionably learning, and the equation of blindness and insight could hardly be plainer. But it works, we note, at a fairly simple narrative level: he learns that Edmond has deceived him. Later, he generalises his experience as Lear does, but in a more flat and prosaic way:

> I stumbled when I saw. Full oft 'tis seen
> Our means secure us, and our mere defects
> Prove our commodities.
> (IV.i. 19–21)

According to Northrop Frye, 'Gloucester's is a morally

intelligible tragedy' in which 'Everything can be explained'.
He adds, 'But the fact that Gloucester's tragedy is morally
explicable goes along with the fact that Gloucester is not the
main character of the play. If we apply such formulae to Lear
they give us very little comfort.'[10] The deaths of the two
characters are strikingly different. Lear's occurs on stage
and, as we will see, none of the witnesses can think of
anything adequate to say about it. Gloucester's is off stage,
and Edgar can describe it in a neat paradox with no stage
reality to contradict or complicate it:

> 　　　his flawed heart—
> Alack, too weak the conflict to support—
> 'Twixt two extremes of passion, joy and grief,
> 　Burst smilingly.
> 　　　　　　　　　　　　　　　　(V.iii. 188–91)

Lear's death resists analysis, resists language itself.
Gloucester's death exists for us *only* as an analysis, a formula
created by Edgar's words.

In Gloucester, then, we see a tragedy that can be
moralised, analysed, explained; and we see a figure who
unquestionably learns, and who moves from blindness to
pained insight and finally to joy.[11] Does Gloucester's
experience give us a simple and clarified version of Lear's to
guide us through its greater complexity, or is it there
essentially as a contrast? Those who want to see the main
story as Lear's redemption will prefer the former reading.
But the contrasts are so striking, and so thoroughly
sustained, that we should probably look to them for a key to
the relationship of the plots, and guide our reading of Lear
accordingly. From the beginning, Gloucester is passive,
worked on by Edmond as he will later be by Edgar. Lear is
active, and precipitates his fall on his own initiative. While
we first see Gloucester in an amiable man-to-man chat with
Kent, Lear is not just centrally placed on his throne but self-
enclosed, self-absorbed. His 'Know that we have divided/In

three our kingdom' (I.i. 37–8) is Lear's *fiat*; this is the voice
of a man who is used to having his words create reality. The
love-test has a superficial air of ceremony but, whereas in a
true ceremony the values of a community are expressed in a
recurring occasion and a set form of words, this 'ceremony'
expresses the needs and desires of one old man, the occasion
is unique, and the speeches have to be made up on the spot.
The principles of ceremony, and the communal stability
they imply, are violated by the demands of Lear's will. As in
the deposition scene in *Richard II*, we see the instruments of
the state being untuned by the King himself. His surrender
of power, however, is more apparent than real. Harry
Berger, Jr, has argued that the terms of his bargain with his
daughters are so one-sided—'all that land and power for a
little rhetorical fluff' — that they will feel in his debt for the
rest of his life; and Cordelia will have the extra burden of
being 'his mother during his second childhood'.[12] Lear
wants, as Alan Sinfield has pointed out, something it is very
difficult for an absolute monarch to have: the assurance 'that
he matters *personally*'.[13] And he intends to matter politically
as well. While the hero of *King Leir* imagines genuine
retreat—'My selfe will sojorne with my sonne of
Cornwall,/And take me to my prayers and my beades' (vi.
556–7)—Lear's train of a hundred knights will mean that he
is always surrounded by an image of power. Even his
division of the kingdom has been seen by Ralph Berry as a
clever strategy of divide and conquer.[14]

From the beginning there is a tension in Lear between the
desire to surrender—'while we/Unburdened crawl toward
death' (I.i. 41–2)—and the desire to cling to power,
authority and love. Yet in clinging to these things Lear
violates them. Richard II gives away his office; Lear splits his
down the middle, separating 'The name and all th'addition
to a king' from 'The sway,/Revenue, execution' (I.i. 136–7).
He is not, we should notice, abdicating. He will be a king
without acting like one, leaving his sons-in-law to act like
kings without being kings. He breaks the integrity of his

office, not giving away his crown, like Richard, but ordering his sons-in-law, 'This crownet part between you' (I.i. 139), leaving us to wonder how such a symbol can be divided. And of course he violates the integrity of love by making it a matter of bargaining. Kingship and love both demand some capacity for surrender: of the man to the office, of the lover to the beloved. Lear, instead, demands to be king on his terms, and to be loved on his terms. Susan Snyder has compared Lear's development to the psychology of dying, which begins with denial: he 'is by no means psychologically ready to yield up power, whatever he says. . . . When he banishes Kent for defending Cordelia, he is exercising automatically, unconsciously, the royal authority he has just supposedly handed over to others'.[15] Even in his act of controlled surrender, Lear in the first scene gives the impression of massive, undisciplined power. But it will not quite do to see him as 'more a magnificent portent than a man'.[16] Beneath the titanic arrogance Lear is vulnerable, anxious, needing to be assured of his future, with the contradictory wants of a child: ease and power, love that is given and love that is secured by being bought. Behind his arrogance lies the simple human fear, Old Adam's fear in *As You Like It* of 'unregarded age in corners thrown' (II.iii. 43). And behind that in turn lies the fear of loneliness and neglect, a fear that can be felt at any age. Lear is not just a foolish old man with everything to learn: some things he knows already, though his way of reacting to that knowledge may be grotesque: that the world is a harsh place even for the powerful, that nature plays vile tricks even on kings, and that the answer is to be found in the nurture and support one gets from other people. Lear enacts, through his contrived drama of surrendering power and finding love, a grotesque parody of the experience he will undergo more seriously in the rest of the play. Monstrously foolish though it is in its context, Lear's question, 'Which of you shall we say doth love us most' (I.i. 51), is not an idle one, and the play will take some pains to give it a proper answer.

But Lear's phrasing is interesting: 'Which of you *shall we say* doth love us most'. The final appeal is to his own judgement. And he seems to have made up his mind already, for he expects Cordelia to give the best speech. The arithmetical logic of the first scene is that once Goneril and Regan's portions have been given out, Cordelia's is already determined. Cordelia's refusal to play the game is the first in a series of moments in which Lear's expectations are frustrated and he has a hard time finding the right reaction. Kent and France try to make him 'See better' (I.i. 158), but they fail. This remains a salient feature of Lear's character throughout: not his openness to new knowledge but his titanic resistance to it. The Leir of the older play is a gentle, mild old man: 'But he, the myrrour of mild patience,/Puts up all wrongs, and never gives reply' (viii. 755–6). When his older daughters turn against him he slips away quietly, unnoticed, in a manner very different from the stormy exits of Shakespeare's Lear. As Shakespeare seems to have created his play's theology (such as it is) by reacting against the sentimental piety of the earlier play, so he seems to have created his hero by reversing the earlier one. Lear's manner in the early scenes is tough and ironic. He appreciates the gruff, self-deprecating humour of the disguised Kent and matches it with his own: 'If thou be'st as poor for a subject as he's for a king, thou'rt poor enough' (I.iv. 21–2). The exchange between the two men displays a style of masculine plain dealing in which Lear is relaxed and self-assured. Above all, he seems to enjoy the *speed* of their exchange. He likes fast decisions, for he does not like to dwell on a subject. It is the slow oily politeness of Goneril that drives him frantic.

At first he simply refuses to see what is happening. The 'great abatement of kindness' his knight perceives becomes in Lear's mind 'a most faint neglect' (I.iv. 58, 66). When he cannot reinterpret, he denies. Confronted with the sight of Kent in the stocks, he refuses to believe it has happened: 'They durst not do't,/They could not, would not do't (II.ii.

199–200 [II.iv]). In a variation on the play's own technique
of visual contradiction, Lear simply refuses to believe what
his eyes, and ours, see all too plainly. When he cannot deny
the facts he still has trouble learning from them. The way
Goneril and Regan have turned against him should have
told him something about the quantifying of love that has
brought him to this pass; but he will not learn. Trying to
assure himself of Regan's love, he puts his clinching
argument last:

> Thou better know'st
> The offices of nature, bond of childhood,
> Effects of courtesy, dues of gratitude.
> Thy half o'th' kingdom hast thou not forgot,
> Wherein I thee endowed.

> (II.ii. 350–4 [II.iv])

His first appeal is to the established and natural connections
of the family, which Cordelia invoked in the first scene: 'I
love your majesty/According to my bond' (I.i. 92–3). In this
view, to violate family ties is to violate a fixed arrangement
that should not depend on individual wills. But Lear, in the
first scene, was not willing to let his daughters' love rest on
that basis: he needed a guarantee he had devised himself.
And it is to that guarantee, 'Thy half o'the kingdom', that he
finally appeals. We see him not advancing towards insight
but retreating from it. As he clings desperately to the
quantifying, bargain-striking view of love, his expression of
it becomes increasingly grotesque: 'Thy fifty yet doth
double five and twenty,/And thou art twice her love' (II.ii.
43–4 [II.iv]). It is as though Lear is trying to prove to himself
that his system works, by stating it in its most absurd form
and continuing stubbornly to believe in it.

When he tries to debate with his daughters, Lear's
argument breaks down just as it is approaching its climax:

O, reason not the need! Our basest beggars
Are in the poorest thing superfluous.
Allow not nature more than nature needs,
Man's life is cheap as beast's. Thou art a lady.
If only to go warm were gorgeous,
Why, nature needs not what thou, gorgeous, wear'st,
Which scarcely keeps thee warm. But for true need—
You heavens, give me that patience, patience I need.
(II.ii. 438–45 [II.iv])

The first part of the speech moves confidently, but when
Lear tries to define 'true need' he breaks off and veers away
from his point. He is in fact defending the superfluity, the
trappings that deck unaccommodated man, which he
himself will reject when he sees Poor Tom. As he describes
Regan's garments his actual contempt for this superfluity
begins to show through, and he seems about to distinguish
between material need and a need for something extra that is
not frivolous, but runs deeper than the material. A need for
what? Presumably something in relations between people:
courtesy, love or respect. But his own thinking is still so
bound by the material, so committed to measuring his
daughters' love by how many knights they will allow him,
that he cannot get this next stage of his argument organised;
and so he breaks off and changes the subject, not to what he
needs from Goneril and Regan but to what he needs from
the heavens.
    At times he hovers on the edge of absurdity:

I have another daughter
Who, I am sure, is kind and comfortable.
When she shall hear this of thee, with her nails
She'll flay thy wolvish visage.
(I.iv. 285–8)

Lear defines kindness as kindness to him; he does not notice
the incongruity this leads to. Rather .than building a

coherent train of thought, he tries out reactions moment by moment, and again this leads to incongruity:

> Thou art a boil,
> A plague-sore or embossèd carbuncle
> In my corrupted blood. But I'll not chide thee.
>
> (II.ii. 396–8 [II.iv])

Yet these moments of absurdity are shot through with moments of insight, some of which are powerfully simple: 'I did her wrong' (I.v. 25). Lear's mind, like the play itself, is constantly on the move, in a dynamic pattern of advance and retreat, surrender and resistance. It is as characteristic of him to fight his feelings as to express them directly.[17] Part of *King Lear*'s overall tension is that while the play as a whole is constantly moving towards new insights, new discoveries, the central character is fighting a tremendous battle *against* knowledge, a battle in which, paradoxically, every loss is an advance.

A related tension is that between Lear's awareness of the world around him and his preoccupation with himself. Goneril's treatment of him leads him to an ironic questioning of his own identity, and the phrasing of his question is revealing:

> Does any here know me? This is not Lear.
> Does Lear walk thus, speak thus? Where are
>   his eyes?
> Either his notion weakens, his discernings
> Are lethargied—ha, waking? 'Tis not so.
> Who is it that can tell me who I am?
>
> *Fool*   Lear's shadow.
>
> (I.iv. 208–13)

We have seen already how problematic identity is in this play, and how the Fool's reply alerts us to the problem. Lear's sense of his identity depends on how other people treat him. If Goneril is not behaving like Lear's daughter, then he must be someone other than Lear. His question is not, who am I, but who is it that can *tell me* who I am? Identity is socially constructed, depending not on oneself but on other people. If Lear is about to start a journey of self-discovery, as his question implies, it will of necessity involve the discovery of other people. And the process works two ways: Lear's view of the rest of the world will be bound up with his sense of himself. As we watch him over the next few scenes, we may wonder whether these two lines of investigation, of the self and of the world, are helping or hindering each other.

One of Lear's achievements is his sudden pity for the Fool in the middle of the storm:

> My wits begin to turn.
> (*To Fool*) Come on, my boy. How dost, my boy? Art
>   cold?
> I am cold myself.—Where is this straw, my fellow?
> The art of our necessities is strange,
> And can make vile things precious. Come, your
>   hovel.—
> Poor fool and knave, I have one part in my heart
> That's sorry yet for thee.
>
>   (III.ii. 67–73)

This is the first time Lear has expressed this kind of feeling for the Fool, indeed the first time in the storm scene that he has noticed him at all. The language is touchingly simple, in stark contrast to the magnificent tirades that have preceded it. The moral he draws about learning to love vile things may refer to the Fool as well as to the hovel. But Lear has discovered pity for the Fool through noticing that he is cold himself, just as he later sympathises with houseless poverty because he himself is houseless, and with Poor Tom because, he insists, his daughters brought him to his pass. In fact, it was not 'Tom's' daughters who brought him to this pass; it was his father. Beneath Tom is Edgar, who has suffered the fate Lear wished on Cordelia. Lear is still better at seeing his sufferings than his offences. His pity for others is real, but it is also a projection of his pity for himself. By the same token, Lear's denunciation of the wickedness of man in the storm scene, though wide-ranging, is focused on one idea: 'all germens spill at once/That makes ingrateful man' (III.ii. 8–9); the centre of humanity's wickedness is what has been done to him. His view of the storm is erratic: he calls on it to aid his curses; he denounces it for joining with his daughters against him. The common factor is that he relates the storm to his own plight. And he can still declare, 'I am a man/More sinned against than sinning' (III.ii. 59–60). In what follows it is the sin of others that continues to preoccupy him.

The treatment he has suffered and the jolting image of humanity Poor Tom presents lead him to ask, as the play itself does, large questions about man and society. His scene with Gloucester is full of broken images of his royal function: we see the king reviewing his troops, receiving homage, dispensing justice. But beneath the trappings of society is the vulnerability Lear has proved in himself:

> When the rain came to wet me once, and the wind to make me chatter; when the thunder would not peace at my bidding, there I found 'em, there I smelt 'em out. Go to, they are not men o' their words. They told me I was everything; 'tis a lie, I am not ague-proof.
>
> (IV.v.100–5 [IV.vi])

In the face of this brute reality all offices are absurd: 'change places and, handy-dandy, which is the justice, which is the thief?' (IV.v. 149–50) [IV.vi]). In his attack on his daughters Lear could not quite bring himself to denounce the superficial trappings of society, for he depended on them himself. Now he sees those trappings not just as superfluous but as deceptive:

Through tattered clothes great vices do appear;
Robes and furred gowns hide all. Plate sin with gold,
And the strong lance of justice hurtles breaks;
Arm it in rags, a pygmy's straw does pierce it.

                                        (IV.v.160–3 [IV.vi])

Lear also recalls Edgar's interpretation of Poor Tom. The animal beneath the robes is not just vulnerable but wicked, and his wickedness is sexual. He begins with a half-recognition of Gloucester:

I pardon that man's life. What was thy cause?
Adultery? Thou shalt not die. Die for adultery!
No, the wren goes to't, and the small gilded fly
Does lecher in my sight. Let copulation thrive,
For Gloucester's bastard son
Was kinder to his father than my daughters
Got 'tween the lawful sheets. To't, luxury, pell-mell,
For I lack soldiers. Behold yon simp'ring dame,
Whose face between her forks presages snow,
That minces virtue, and does shake the head
To hear of pleasure's name.
The fitchew nor the soilèd horse goes to't
With a more riotous appetite. Down from the waist
They're centaurs, though women all above.
But to the girdle do the gods inherit;
Beneath is all the fiend's. There's hell, there's darkness,
there is the sulphurous pit, burning, scalding, stench,
consumption. Fie, fie, fie; pah, pah! Give me an ounce of
civet, good apothecary, sweeten my imagination.

                                        (IV.v. 109–27 [IV.vi]

Gloucester's offence was adultery, and Lear begins with that. While Edgar will later see this as a crime deserving the punishment of blindness, Lear excuses it with ironic tolerance: man is simply doing what the animals do. Why should one expect him to be different? Besides, the world

must be peopled; for one thing, Lear's supply of knights is
low: 'I lack soldiers'. But then the thought of the animal in
man produces a sudden wave of disgust, in the image of the
simpering dame. Initially, her offence seems to be not
sexuality but the desire to conceal it. Even that degree of
tolerance breaks, as sexuality itself becomes disgusting. We
may have no glimpse of heaven in this play, but we do have a
glimpse of hell: it lies, in Lear's imagination, between a
woman's legs. Then Lear seems to decide that the fault lies
not in humanity, but in his way of looking at humanity: it is
his imagination, not the body, that is corrupt. Gloucester
the adulterer, who began this train of thought, becomes the
apothecary who must end it by curing Lear's diseased
imagination. Gloucester tries, not to cure Lear, but simply
to honour him: 'O, let me kiss that hand!' The fact that the
gesture is physical recalls Lear's insight that beneath the
trappings of society is the reality of the body, and leads to
his final statement of the body's corruption: 'Let me wipe it
first; it smells of mortality' (IV.v. 128–9 [IV.iv]). We go
from the stench of sex to the stench of death. The general
impression of the speech is not of secure insight but of a
restless probing, excited and urgent, attacking and recoiling,
moving through a series of self-contradictions, as the mind
shrinks from the unbearable, then dares itself to face it, then
turns away again.

Lear's insights into the corruption of justice and the
foulness of sexuality fuse into a single image:

> Thou rascal beadle, hold thy bloody hand.
> Why dost thou lash that whore? Strip thine own back.
> Thou hotly lusts to use her in that kind
> For which thou whip'st her.
>
> (IV.v. 156–9 [IV.vi])

In this, one of Lear's most dreadful images, lust and cruelty
seem to operate not just beneath the system of justice but
through it. Yet this leads Lear not to a universal

denunciation of man, like the one heard in the storm scene,
but to a universal tolerance: 'None does offend, none, I say
none' (IV.v. 164 [IV.vi]). He has passed beyond his casual
tolerance of sex as something the animals do, to a bitter
equivalent of Cordelia's 'no cause, no cause'. This
forgiveness comes not through wiping out offences but
through seeing them as universal. None does offend,
because all are equally guilty. From this wide general insight
Lear's mind suddenly snaps back to the particular: he
recognises the old man who is clumsily pulling off his boots
and crying like a baby. As Gloucester has said to Edgar,
'Take my purse', Lear makes a more basic offer:

> If thou wilt weep my fortunes, take my eyes.
> I know thee well enough; thy name is Gloucester.
> Thou must be patient. We came crying hither.
> Thou know's the first time that we smell the air
> We waul and cry.
>
> (IV.v. 172–6 [IV.vi])

Universal sin has become universal suffering; we are back
from the wicked animal to the naked one. The first
symptom of life is a cry. And as the image of the weeping old
man fuses with that of the crying baby, the whole of human
life becomes a circle of pain that closes in a moment.

In much of this Lear's mind seems to have gone well
beyond his own personal misfortunes. He is looking out at
the world. But he offers his eyes to Gloucester on condition:
'If thou wilt keep my fortunes, take my eyes'. He is still
bargaining, and his bargains still have reference to himself.
We may wonder why he is so concerned with sex, since—
unlike Troilus or Othello—he has not suffered betrayal in
this area of his life. The answer may lie back in the storm
sequence: 'Judicious punishment: 'twas this flesh
begot/Those pelican daughters' (III.iv. 70–1). As a king
exiled in his own land, Lear sees through the systems of
power and justice that he used to administer. As a betrayed

father, he sees beneath parenthood the sulphurous pit from
which we all spring. Broad though it is, his vision is finally
bordered by what has happened to him. Throughout his
scene with Gloucester, from 'every inch a king' to 'None
does offend . . . I'll able 'em' (IV.v. 107, 164 [IV.vi]), Lear
insists on his own authority. And his view of universal
corruption, as I have already suggested, finds no place for
what we see all round him: images of loyalty and love, a son
helping a father, an old blind courtier trying to honour a
fallen king, an army led by his daughter coming to his
rescue. Lear himself participates in this kindness, showing
that there is more to parenthood than propagated curse.
Comforting the crying Gloucester, he is like a parent
tending a child. As the two old men cling together, all Edgar
can do is stand back and comment lamely, 'O, matter and
impertinency mixed—/Reason in madness' (IV.v. 170–1
[IV.vi]), as though to emphasise that no commentary can do
justice to this picture of the human bond. Yet this
achievement is not fixed, any more than earlier ones have
been. In a moment the old cursing, vengeful Lear is back:
'when I have stol'n upon these son-in-laws,/Then kill, kill,
kill, kill, kill!' (IV.v. 182–3 [IV.vi]). We are right back to the
Lear of the first two acts, who could think of nothing better
to do than get even; and his vengeance is pointlessly
misdirected, for one son-in-law is dead and the other is on
his side.

It is at this point that Cordelia's attendants come to rescue
him. Lear runs away from them. Waking in Cordelia's tent,
he gets what he wanted in the first scene: 'I . . . thought to set
my rest/On her kind nursery'(I.i. 123–4). Yet once again he
resists, fighting off comfort as he had fought off knowledge.
Cordelia addresses him with titles of respect, 'How does my
royal lord? How fares your majesty?', to which he replies by
trying to put as much distance between them as he can:

You do me wrong to take me out o'th' grave.
Thou art a soul in bliss, but I am bound

Upon a wheel of fire, that mine own tears
Do scald like molten lead.

(IV.vi. 37–41 [IV.vii])

What we see is a daughter tending a father, a basic image of
human kindness that echoes Lear's comforting of
Gloucester and the Fool, and Edgar's taking Gloucester by
the hand. What Lear sees is the unbridgeable gulf between
heaven and hell. And while he is offered new life, in images
of restoration (music and fresh garments) that will be used
again in Shakespeare's final romances, his first reaction is
resentment at being brought out of the grave.[18] Even as he
gropes to understand his new experience, old ways of
thought cling to him. He still imagines a scheme of
retribution, the difference being that he is the offender who
must be punished: 'If you have poison for me, I will drink it'
(IV.vi. 65 [IV.vii]). He seeks physical guarantees of the
reality of this experience, and they are images of suffering: 'I
feel this pin prick'; 'Be your tears wet? Yes, faith' (IV.vi. 49,
64 [IV.vii]). He cannot accept this experience as real unless
there is some pain in it.

Cordelia has a moment of shyness at Lear's waking. As he
sleeps she kisses him, and speaks eloquently of her pity and
her desire to restore him. but when he wakes her first
impulse is to ask her attendant to speak to him, and he has to
tell her, 'Madam, do you; 'tis fittest' (IV.vi. 36 [IV.vii]). We
go for a moment back to the first scene, to Cordelia's
reluctance to speak, her fear that her language cannot match
the occasion. But this time her presence—for when she
speaks, her words are few and simple and Lear never replies
to them directly—is enough to guide him out of the abyss.
We return to the first scene in another respect: this time
Lear really does give away his kingship. He refuses to
acknowledge the titles she uses, and when told he is in his
own kingdom replies, 'Do not abuse me' (IV.vi. 71 [IV.vii]).
And he has, at last, an answer to his question, 'Which of you
shall we say doth love us most'. He gropes for an answer to

his other key question: 'Who is it that can tell me who I am?'
His own attempts to establish his identity are fumbling.
Having seen the body as the essential reality of man, he now
finds his own body unfamiliar: 'I will not swear these are my
hands' (IV.vi. 48 [IV.vii]). The body is not, perhaps, our
final reality after all. The fresh clothes, which in Geoffrey of
Monmouth and Holinshed are given to him so that he will
make a respectable appearance before Cordelia's husband,
and which here are images of restoration and new life, not
designed to impress in a worldly way—these clothes are
simply disorientating: 'all the skill I have/Remembers not
these garments' (IV.vi. 59–60 [IV.vii]). As before, clothing
seems unnatural; but while previously Lear could denounce
it as superfluous or deceptive, now it is simply puzzling. In
his earlier tirades, he was grandly unaware of his own
absurdity. Now, with nothing absurd about him, he asks
shyly, 'Pray do not mock'; 'Do not laugh at me' (IV.vi. 52,
61 [IV.vii]). The old self-assertiveness is gone.

The difficulty of fixing an identity, which is part of our
experience of responding to the play, is now embodied in
Lear, who seems to himself, perhaps for the first time, to be
truly Lear's shadow. He never does succeed in naming
himself. In fact, for the rest of the play he never speaks his
own name. The identity he finds for himself is both a plain
but generalised recognition of present reality and a startling
change from the proud, raging Lear of the earlier scenes:

> I am a very foolish, fond old man.
> Fourscore and upward,
> Not an hour more nor less; and to deal plainly
> I fear I am not in my perfect mind.
>
> (IV.vi. 53–6 [IV.vii])

Shy and apologetic, trying to kneel before his daughter, he
seems more the meek Leir of the earlier play than
Shakespeare's hero. In his confrontation with Goneril he
affected not to recognize her—'Your name, fair

gentlewoman?' (I.iv. 214)—as part of his ironic questioning
of his own identity. Now he is genuinely unsure of himself,
and when he finally gropes to an act of recognition, of
naming, it is not himself he names:

> Do not laugh at me,
> For as I am a man, I think this lady
> To be my child, Cordelia.
>
> (IV.vi. 61–3 [IV.vii])

From this point he remembers what has happened to him,
and what he has done; and some of his old habits of mind,
particularly his view of human relations as a matter of
bargaining and exchange, begin to reassert themselves:

> I know you do not love me; for your sisters
> Have, as I do remember, done me wrong.
> You have some cause; they have not.
>
> (IV.vi. 66–8 [IV.vii])

'I know you do not love me' shows him in some danger of
repeating his old mistake about Cordelia; but at least he is
re-establishing some sense of his identity, not through
counting up the number of knights he is allowed, or noting
gestures of respect (he rejects those) but simply through an
awareness that he has a relationship with Cordelia. In a
tentative way, he learns something from her. His reply to
her 'No cause, no cause' is a *non sequitur*, 'Am I in France?'
(IV.vi. 68–9 [IV.vii]). But the idea of forgiveness has been
planted in this mind, and he returns to it at the end of the
scene, asking her to do what she has already done: 'You
must bear with me. Pray you now, forget/And forgive. I am
old and foolish' (IV.vi. 76–7 [IV.vii]).

In the way it seems to resolve questions raised in the first
scene, and to give a true image of what was parodied there—
Lear shedding his kingship, to be tended by his youngest
daughter—Act 4 Scene 6 could be an ending. Lear's

achievement of humility seems a final breakthrough. So
does his critical awareness of himself, based on his
recognition of Cordelia ('You have some cause') and leading
to his simple plea for forgiveness. But this is not altogether a
new Lear. Part of what makes the scene convincing, and
therefore moving, is that Lear is still, as he has always been, a
slow learner. He gropes reluctantly towards his new life,
trying at first to cling to the old certainties of pain and
punishment. His expressions of new insight are tentative
and incomplete. This includes his insight into himself: 'old
and foolish' does not quite sum up the character we have
seen or the reasons he needs forgiveness. And from this
point in the play his mind contracts as sharply as it had
expanded. He ceases to care about kingship, justice or
power. Only one thing matters: Cordelia. Not even love, as
an idea, matters; simply Cordelia. He is beyond
abstractions. His entire life now hinges on one person. And
about her he has one thing left to learn.

In watching the reunion, we hardly notice the acute
contraction of Lear's mind, for his new experience seems so
complete in itself. But when he next appears we are bound to
notice. Lear is quite happy to have lost the battle and to be
sent to prison so long as Cordelia is with him:

> Come, let's away to prison.
> We two alone will sing like birds i'th' cage.
> When thou dost ask me blessing, I'll kneel down
> And ask of thee forgiveness; so we'll live,
> And pray, and sing, and tell old tales, and laugh
> At gilded butterflies, and hear poor rogues
> Talk of court news, and we'll talk with them too—
> Who loses and who wins, who's in, who's out,
> And take upon's the mystery of things
> As if we were God's spies; and we'll wear out
> In a walled prison packs and sects of great ones
> That ebb and flow by th'moon.
>					(V.iii. 8–19)

Questions like 'Who loses and who wins, who's in, who's out' were once of vital importance to him, for he was in the thick of such action himself. Now, in line with his rejection of kingship in his previous scene, he views the whole of public life with detached amusement. Even the notion of being God's spy does not imply judgement or insight; merely the detachment of a god who finds his creatures laughable—not unlike Gloucester's gods, who kill men for their sport. Yet we know that Lear cannot live like this. Cordelia's question, 'Shall we not see these daughters and these sisters?' (V.iii. 7) shows her awareness of political reality; and that reality, in the form of Edmond and his army, is on stage with Lear even as he speaks, theatrically contradicting his words. Who loses and who wins is not an idle question, but a question of life and death: Edmond has announced his intention of having Lear and Cordelia killed if they lose the battle, and in a few moments he will give the order.

Barbara Everett has noted the childlike, unreal quality of Lear's vision,[19] and W. F. Blissett observes the irony that Lear 'has not resigned the joys of resignation'.[20] Perhaps the most insidious danger in the speech is the way Lear turns his own relations with Cordelia into a childlike game of make-believe, kneeling and forgiving as they did at their reunion. We cannot blame Lear for wanting to hold on to that scene, but the cost of repeating it instead of letting it go is to devalue and trivialise it. As so often, Lear wants to hold back while the play moves on. As he imagined the gods aiding his curses, he now imagines them giving their blessing to his life with Cordelia. But his own imagination starts to send out warning signals:

> Upon such sacrifices, my Cordelia,
> The gods themselves throw incense. Have I caught
>   thee?
> He that parts us shall bring a brand from heaven
> And fire us hence like foxes.
>   (V.iii. 20–3)

The reference to incense implies a sacrifice on an altar, Lear
and Cordelia going through a kind of death. It is a sanctified
death, in which they will go together to a new life. But one
worry still haunts him: they could be parted. Picking up the
image of the sacrifice on the altar, he insists that only fire
from heaven could do it. For a moment we glimpse an image
of frightened, tortured animals, taking us back to the play's
middle scenes. Lear insists that he is describing an
impossibility, something that cannot happen. Yet we see in a
moment that it will not need fire from heaven to part them;
it needs only Edmond giving an order to his captain. The
ordinary world, that Lear finds so comically distant, closes
in and destroys him.

And so we return to the death of Cordelia. Lear resists it,
as he has always resisted new knowledge. He kills the captain
who is hanging her, and throughout his last moments he
alternates between stark recognition—

> She's gone forever.
> I know when one is dead and when one lives.
> She's dead as earth.
>
> (V.iii. 234–6)

—and refusal:

> This feather stirs. She lives. If it be so,
> It is a chance which does redeem all sorrows
> That ever I have felt.
>
> (V.iii. 240–2)

Whatever we may have felt about Lear's earlier resistance to
knowledge, we are with him here. His struggle between
acceptance and refusal of this unbearable fact is our struggle
as well. Lear's knowledge has never been the full knowledge
of the play: we have always been able to see more than he
does. But Lear's experience, of struggling bewildered
through shock after shock, has been like our experience of

the play, and here we are close to being one with him. We have already seen how many readers have in their own ways refused to accept the death of Cordelia.

But we feel its inevitably, not just in the way the last scene echoes and completes the first, but in the way images from all over the play come crashing down on us in Lear's last speech:

> And my poor fool is hanged! No, no, no life?
> Why should a dog, a horse, a rat have life,
> And thou no breath at all? Thou'lt come no more.
> Never, never, never, never, never.
> (*To Kent*) Pray you, undo this button. Thank you, sir.
>
> (V.iii. 281–6)

The Fool, the animals of the middle scenes, Lear's attempts to strip, the service he gets from his attendants, all find echoes here.It is as though the whole play is bearing down on him, and on us. Yet Lear's actual death seems to have given Shakespeare trouble, for it is at this point that we have the most striking and significant change between the Quarto and the Folio. Here is the Quarto version:

> Lear   . . . Pray you, undo
>   This button. Thank you, sir. O, O, O, O!
> Edgar   He faints. (*To Lear*) My lord, my lord!
> Lear   Break, heart, I prithee break.
> Edgar   Look up, my lord.
> Kent   Vex not his ghost. O, let him pass.
>
> (Q.xxiv. 303–8)

Lear seems to will his heart—the 'rising heart' of his exchange with the Fool (II.ii. 292–6 [IV.iv])—to break. His death is centred on his own feeling, his own pain; he is terribly aware of that pain, and consciously uses it to bring on death. If this were the only version of the scene we had,

we would accept its terrible logic as a fitting end for Lear.
But the Folio goes beyond it:

> Lear   . . . Pray you, undo this button. Thank you,
>   sir.
>   Do you see this? Look on her. Look, her
>   lips.
>   Look there, look there.   *He dies.*
> Edgar   He faints. (*To Lear*) My lord, my lord!
> Kent   (*to Lear*) Break, heart, I prithee break.
> Edgar   (*to Lear*)   Look up, my lord.
> Kent   Vex not his ghost. O, let him pass.
>
> (V.iii. 285–9)

Lear does not even know he is dying;[21] his focus is on
Cordelia. Once again our experience corresponds to his: the
death that preoccupies us in the last scene is not the death of
the hero: it is Cordelia's death, to which he is 'hardly more
than a needful afterthought'.[22] As he found his identity in
her, he finds his death in hers. It is the play's last and most
painful image of the human bond. Less directly than Edgar,
but just as decisively, Cordelia has killed her father.

Yet this does affirm something about Cordelia, and about
humanity. Certainly not in any hope of immortality; there is
no suggestion of that.[23] Nor, I think, in Bradley's notion that
Lear thinks he sees returning life on Cordelia's lips. If he
dies of joy it is at best a merciful delusion, a cheat like
Gloucester's fall. More to the point, we do not know what
Lear sees on Cordelia's lips: we register instead the fact of
his concentration on them. The range of his mind has
narrowed all through the last scenes, from humanity to
Cordelia, and now it contracts to a single intense point:
Cordelia's lips. The lips that kissed him as he slept, from
which he wanted eloquent words in the first scene, from
which he now wants merely breath. We do not know
whether he sees life or death there; it is the concentration
that matters. An actor could play unbearable joy, or

unbearable grief, and be true to the scene either way. Lear's commitment to Cordelia is so intense that it ends his life, demonstrating her value to him with terrible decisiveness, and countering Lear's savage view of man in the middle scenes. If man were just a bare forked animal or a wicked animal, it would not matter, as it so painfully does, that a dog, a horse or a rat should live and that Cordelia should die.[24] Lear has learnt not just how much Cordelia loves him but how much he loves her, and this knowledge kills him. If this is an affirmation, it is an affirmation that comes not in spite of pain, but through it.

The survivors try for other kinds of affirmation. Albany wants the Tate ending:

> What comfort to this great decay may come
> Shall be applied; for us, we will resign
> During the life of this old majesty
> To him our absolute power. . . .
>   All friends shall taste
> The wages of their virtue, and all foes
> The cup of their deservings.—O see, see!
>   (V.iii. 273–80)

Albany's words break off as he confronts the sight of Lear with the dead Cordelia; it is as though he can make this speech only by turning away from the reality on which our own eyes are fixed, and when he turns back he breaks down. Edgar's 'Look up, my lord' (V.iii. 288) recalls his attempt to comfort Gloucester at Dover, and earns Kent's rebuke. Comfort is not just irrelevant but cruel; Lear needs to die. And the play's last speeches are shaken, feeble, deliberately inadequate, as though in the end 'language as literature, therefore language at the top of its bent, declares itself inadequate for the task it has just performed':[25]

> *Albany*   . . . Friends of my soul, you twain
>   Rule in this realm, and the gored state sustain.

Kent	I have a journey, sir, shortly to go:
	My master calls me; I must not say no.
Edgar	The weight of this sad time we must obey,
	Speak what we feel, not what we ought to
	say.
	The oldest hath borne most. We that are
	young
	Shall never see so much, nor live so long.

(V.iii. 295–302)

There is no Fortinbras or Malcolm here to order the state
and see that life goes on. The kingdom that Lear grandly
sliced in three, and then in two, now lies in ruin, and no one
feels like picking through the rubble. Albany wants no part
of worldly power; Kent wants no part of life. Edgar seems
prepared to confront only the present experience, feels that
something ought to be at least *said* about it, but does not
know what to say. He ends the play with what sounds like a
lame tribute to the endurance and longevity of the old, and a
fear that his own life may be shorter. (This may touch on the
belief current in Shakespeare's time that the world was in its
last days, one evidence for this being that modern men did
not live as long as the patriarchs.) But what Edgar's halting
words really convey, through their sheer inarticulateness, is
an admission that Lear's experience, and to a lesser extent
Gloucester's, have been larger and deeper than his own
thoughts can compass. We cannot, finally, cope with this
ending through discursive language any more than Edgar
can. We have to face instead the thing itself, embodied in the
stage picture of Lear with the dead Cordelia.

Lear is not so much a character who has been saved or
educated as a character who has been through an intense
experience, one that has presented him—and us—with basic
images of the human condition, hurled at us with brutal
speed and impact: the naked madman, the crying baby, the
soul in bliss, the dead child. His death is the completion of a
life lived at the extreme. That sense of extremity has been

created by collisions between language and experience, as the characters confront an intractable world. If Lear seems the grandest of them, it is because he puts up the most titanic resistance to that world. But this final experience, Cordelia's death, is so intense that it kills him. For us that experience is the play's final reality, after which the efforts of language fade and die. But the image, as stubborn and intractable as Lear himself, survives to haunt us. Asserting his power over his own life, Lear began the play by asking his daughters to say how much they loved him. He ends by demonstrating his own love, and our mortal helplessness, in a manner beyond words.

Notes

CHAPTER 1

1. *Johnson on Shakespeare*, edited by Walter Raleigh (reprint Oxford University Press, Oxford, 1925), pp. 161–2.
2. *King Lear: Text and Performance* (Macmillan, London, 1984), p. 39.
3. See Stephen Booth, *King Lear, Macbeth, Indefinition, and Tragedy* (Yale University Press, New Haven and London, 1983), pp. 6–11.
4. *Shakespearean Tragedy* (reprint Macmillan, London, 1957), pp. 206–7.
5. *King Lear in Our Time* (University of California Press, Berkeley and Los Angeles, 1965), p. 65. Mack gives a full discussion of the play's use of pastoral conventions, pp. 63–6.
6. *Indefinition*, pp. 61–78.
7. *The Comic Matrix of Shakespeare's Tragedies* (Princeton University Press, Princeton, 1979), p. 139. Her entire discussion (pp. 136–79) should be read by anyone interested in *King Lear's* affinity with the comedies.
8. Nahum Tate, *The History of King Lear*, in *Shakespeare Adaptations*, edited by Montague Summers (reprint Benjamin Blom, New York, and London 1966), p. 253.

9. *Shakespearean Tragedy*, p. 241.
10. *Patterns in Shakespearian Tragedy* (Methuen, London, 1960), p. 122.
11. For a fuller survey see Nicholas Brooke, 'The Ending of *King Lear*', in *Shakespeare 1564–1964*, edited by Edward A. Bloom (Brown University Press, Providence, 1964), pp. 71–87 (pp. 71–7).
12. Relevant extracts from these and other sources, and a full text of *King Leir*, are found in *Narrative and Dramatic Sources of Shakespeare*, edited by Geoffrey Bullough, VII (Routledge & Kegan Paul, London; and Columbia University Press, New York, 1973). All references to source material are to this edition.
13. See Booth, *Indefinition*, p. 24. On the play's use of silence, see Jill Levenson, 'What the Silence Said: Still Points in "King Lear" ', in *Shakespeare 1971*, edited by Clifford Leech and J.M.R. Margeson (University of Toronto Press, Toronto and Buffalo, 1972), pp. 215–29.
14. 'Visual Contradiction in *King Lear*', *Shakespeare Quarterly* 21 (1970) 491–5. Hargreaves is not the only critic to have discussed this effect, but we may credit him with finding a useful label for it.
15. See James Black, ' "King Lear": Art Upside-Down', *Shakespeare Survey* 33 (1980) 35–42 (p. 39).
16. Bradley, *Shakespearean Tragedy*, p. 202.
17. 'The Blinding of 'Gloster', *Review of English Studies* 21 (1945) 264–70 (p. 267).
18 *Acting and Action in Shakespearean Tragedy* (Princeton University Press, Princeton, 1985), pp. 72–3. Harley Granville-Barker notes that Lear's 'hands are at play all the time with actual things'. See *Prefaces to Shakespeare*, I (reprint Princeton University Press, Princeton, 1952), p. 281.
19. *Shakespearean Tragedy*, pp. 210–11.
20. *The Lear World: A Study of King Lear in its Dramatic Context* (University of Toronto Press, Toronto and Buffalo, 1977), pp. 47–55.

21. *Johnson on Shakespeare*, p. 161.
22. For a full discussion of morality-play influence on *King Lear*, see Mack, *King Lear in Our Time*, pp. 56–63.
23. *The Wheel of Fire*, 4th edition (reprint Methuen, London, 1960), p. 177.
24. *Patterns*, pp. 134, 135.
25. *Shakespeare's Doctrine of Nature* (Faber, London, 1961), p. 175.
26. *Radical Tragedy* (Harvester, Brighton; and University of Chicago Press, Chicago, 1984), p. 197.
27. *Some Shakespearean Themes* (reprint Penguin, Harmondsworth, 1966), p. 77. For a full discussion, see Danby, *Doctrine of Nature*, *passim*.
28. 'Lear and Laing', *Essays in Criticism* 26 (1976) 1–16 (p.16).
29. See William R. Elton, *King Lear and the Gods* (Huntington Library, San Marino, 1966), p. 201.
30. See Lillian Feder, *Madness in Literature* (Princeton University Press, Princeton, 1980), p. 146.
31. *King Lear in Our Time*, p. 111.
32. *Some Shakespearean Themes*, p. 79. See also Snyder, *Comic Matrix*, p. 179.
33. Mary Lascelles has made an interesting case for seeing doom paintings, like the one in the Guild Chapel at Stratford upon Avon, as one source for the play. See ' "King Lear" and Doomsday', *Shakespeare Survey* 26 (1973) 69–79.
34. See René E. Fortin, 'Hermeneutical Circularity and Christian Interpretations of *King Lear*', *Shakespeare Studies* 12 (1979) 113–25 (pp. 118–19).
35. *This Great Stage: Image and Structure in King Lear* (reprint University of Washington Press, Seattle, 1963), p. 278.
36. Brooke, 'Ending', p. 84.
37. *Patterns*, pp. 130–1.
38. 'King Lear and His Comforters', *Essays in Criticism* 16 (1966) 135–46 (p. 139).

39. '*King Lear*: The Lear Family Romance', *Centennial Review* 23 (1979) 348–76 (p. 363).
40. 'Ending', p. 78.
41. Goldman, *Acting and Action*, p. 90.
42. *Shakespeare's Revision of King Lear* (Princeton University Press, Princeton, 1980), p. 55.
43. *Johnson on Shakespeare*, pp. 159–60.

CHAPTER 2

1. *King Lear in Our Time* (University of California Press, Berkeley and Los Angeles, 1965), p. 90.
2. Long before Brook's production, Harley Granville-Barker pointed out that Lear really is stubborn and disruptive, and his knights really must have been a nuisance; see *Prefaces to Shakespeare*, I (reprint Princeton University Press, Princeton, 1952), p. 286. For a contrary view, see Mack, *King Lear in Our Time*, pp. 30–2.
3. 'The Politics of *King Lear*', in *Essays on Literature and Society* (Hogarth Press, London, 1949), pp. 31–48 (pp. 41–2).
4. *Prefaces to Shakespeare*, I, p. 291.
5. See Rosalie L. Cólie, 'Reason and Need: *King Lear* and the "Crisis" of the Aristocracy', in *Some Facets of King Lear: Essays in Prismatic Criticism*, edited by Rosalie L. Colie and F.T. Flahiff (University of Toronto Press, Toronto, 1974), pp. 185–219 (p. 208).
6. *Shakespearean Tragedy* (reprint Macmillan, London, 1957), p. 251.
7. *Johnson on Shakespeare*, edited by Walter Raleigh (reprint Oxford University Press, Oxford, 1925), p. 158.
8. *Shakespearean Tragedy*, p. 257.
9. See Granville-Barker, *Prefaces*, I, p. 307.

10. See Steven Urkowitz, *Shakespeare's Revision of King Lear* (Princeton University Press, Princeton, 1980), pp. 91–2.
11. *King Lear, Macbeth, Indefinition, and Tragedy* (Yale University Press, New Haven and London, 1983), p. 46.
12. *Prefaces*, I, p. 274.
13. *Lear's Self-Discovery* (University of California Press, Berkeley and Los Angeles; and Cambridge University Press, Cambridge, 1967), p. 88.
14. *Madness in Literature* (Princeton University Press, Princeton, 1980), p. 133.
15. *The Masks of King Lear* (University of California Press, Berkeley, Los Angeles and London, 1972), pp. 218, 263.
16. See, for example, David Pirie, 'Lear as King', *Critical Quarterly* 22 (1980) 5–20 (p. 19).
17. *An Essay on King Lear* (Cambridge University Press, Cambridge, 1974), p. 116.
18. *Shakespearean Tragedy*, p. 268.
19. *Coleridge on Shakespeare*, edited by Terence Hawkes (Penguin, Harmondsworth. 1969), p. 203.
20. Kathleen McLuskie complains that Act 4 Scene 3, by the way it introduces the reunion, 'substitutes the pleasure of pathos for suspense' and 'closes off any response other than complete engagement with the characters' emotions'; see 'The Patriarchal Bard: Feminist Criticism and Shakespeare: *King Lear* and *Measure for Measure*', in *Political Shakespeare*, edited by Jonathan Dollimore and Alan Sinfield (Manchester University Press, Manchester; and Cornell University Press, Ithaca and London, 1985), 88–108 (p. 101). She does not note the effect of the Folio cut.

CHAPTER 3

1. *Criticism as Dialogue* (Cambridge University Press, Cambridge, 1969), p. 113.

2. *This Great Stage: Image and Structure in King Lear* (reprint University of Washington Press, Seattle, 1963), p. 270.

3. *Shakespearean Tragedy* (Reprint Macmillan, London, 1957), p. 235.

4. *The Wheel of Fire*, 4th edition (reprint Methuen, London, 1960), p. 179.

5. *Patterns in Shakespearean Tragedy* (Methuen, London, 1960), p. 116.

6. *Radical Tragedy* (Brighton, Harvester; and Chicago, University of Chicago Press, 1984), pp. 193, 195.

7. 'The New King Lear', *Critical Quarterly* 2 (1960) 325–39 (p. 335).

8. *Some Shakespearean Themes* (reprint Penguin, Harmondsworth, 1966), p. 80

9. *An Essay on King Lear* (Cambridge University Press, Cambridge, 1974), p. 68.

10. *Fools of Time: Studies in Shakespearean Tragedy* (University of Toronto Press, Toronto, Buffalo and London, 1967), pp. 113–14.

11. On the relationship between the two plots, see Bridget Gellert Lyons, 'The Subplot as Simplification in *King Lear*', in *Some Facets of King Lear: Essay in Prismatic Criticisim*, edited by Rosalie L. Colie and F.T. Flahiff (University of Toronto Press, Toronto and Buffalo, 1974), pp. 23–38.

12. '*King Lear*: The Lear Family Romance', *Centennial Review* 23 (1979) 348–76 (pp. 354, 355).

13. 'Lear and Laing', *Essays in Criticism* 26 (1976) 1–16 (p. 3).

14. 'Lear's System', *Shakespeare Quarterly* 35 (1984) 421–9 (pp. 422–6).

15. '*King Lear* and the Psychology of Dying', *Shakespeare Quarterly* 3 (1982) 449–60 (p. 455).

16. Harley Granville-Barker, *Prefaces to Shakespeare*, I (reprint Princeton University Press, Princeton, 1952), p. 285.

17. See Michael Goldman, *Acting and Action in*

Shakespearean Tragedy (Princeton University Press, Princeton, 1985), p. 77.

18. Marvin Rosenberg, in *The Masks of King Lear* (University of California Press, Berkeley, Los Angeles and London, 1972), reports John Gielgud's playing of this scene: he 'was bewildered, troubled, he was fretful—even at first 'a bit sulky,' as per Granville-Barker's direction' (p. 286).

19. 'The New King Lear', p. 332–3.

20. 'Recognition in *King Lear*', in *Some Facets*, pp. 103–16 (p. 113).

21. See F.T. Flahiff, 'Edgar: Once and Future King', in *Some Facets*, pp. 221–37 (p.232).

22. Maynard Mack, *King Lear in Our Time* (University of California Press, Berkeley and Los Angeles, 1965), p. 84.

23. See William R. Elton, *King Lear and the Gods* (Huntington Library, San Marino, 1966), pp. 54–5.

24. See Paul A. Jorgensen, *Lear's Self-Discovery* (University of California Press, Berkeley and Los Angeles; and Cambridge University Press, Cambridge, 1967), p. 124.

25. Sheldon P. Zitner, '*King Lear* and Its Language', in *Some Facets*, pp. 3–22 (p. 4).

Bibliography

Berger, Harry Jr, 'King Lear; The Lear Family Romance',
    Centennial Review 23 (1979) 348–76.
Berry, Ralph, 'Lear's System', Shakespeare Quaterly 35
    (1984) 421–9.
Black, James, ' "King Lear": Art Upside-Down',
    Shakespeare Survey 33 (1980) 35–42.
Booth, Stephen, King Lear, Macbeth, Indefinition and
    Tragedy (Yale University Press, New Haven and
    London, 1983).
Bradley, A.C. Shakespearean Tragedy (reprint Macmillan,
    London, 1957).
Brooke, Nicholas, 'The Ending of King Lear', in Edward A.
    Bloom (ed.) Shakespeare 1954–1964 (Brown University
    Press, Providence, 1964), pp. 71–87.
Bullough, Geoffrey (ed.), Narrative and Dramatic Sources of
    Shakespeare, Vol. 7 (Routledge & Kegan Paul, London;
    and Columbia University Press, New York, 1973).
Coleridge on Shakespeare, ed. Terence Hawkes (Penguin,
    Harmondsworth, 1969).
Colie, Rosalie L. and Flahiff, F.T. (eds.) Some Facets of King
    Lear: Essays in Prismatic Criticism (University of
    Toronto Press, Toronto and Buffalo, 1974).
Danby, John F., Shakespeare's Doctrine of Nature (Faber &
    Faber, London, 1961).

Dollimore, Jonathan, *Radical Tragedy* (Harvester, Brighton, and University of Chicago Press, Chicago, 1984).

Elton, William R., *King Lear and the Gods* (Huntington Library, San Marino, 1966).

Everett, Barbara, 'The New King Lear', *Critical Quarterly* 2 (1960) 325–39.

Feder, Lillian, *Madness in Literature* (Princeton University Press, Princeton, 1980).

Fly, Richard, *Shakespeare's Mediated World* (University of Massachusetts Press, Amherst, 1976).

Fortin, René E., 'Hermeneutical Circularity and Christian Interpretations of *King Lear*', *Shakespeare Studies* 12 (1979) 113–25.

Frye, Northrop, *Fools of Time: Studies in Shakespearean Tragedy* (University of Toronto Press, Toronto, Buffalo and London, 1967).

Goldberg, S.L., *An Essay on King Lear* (Cambridge University Press, Cambridge 1974).

Goldman, Michael, *Acting and Action in Shakespearean Tragedy* (Princeton University Press, Princeton, 1985).

Granville-Barker, Harley, *Prefaces to Shakespeare*, Vol. 1 (reprint Princeton University Press, Princeton, 1952).

Hargreaves, H.A., 'Visual Contradiction in *King Lear*', *Shakespeare Quarterly*, 21 (1970), 491–5.

Heilman, Robert Bechtold, *This Great Stage: Image and Structure in King Lear* (reprint University of Washington Press, Seattle, 1963).

Johnson on Shakespeare, ed. Walter Raleigh (reprint Oxford University Press, Oxford, 1925).

Jorgensen, Paul A., *Lear's Self-Discovery* (University of California Press, Berkeley and Los Angeles; and Cambridge University Press, Cambridge, 1967)

Knight, G. Wilson, *The Wheel of Fire*, 4th edition (reprint Methuen, London, 1960).

Knights, L.C., *Some Shakespearean Themes* (reprint Penguin, Harmondsworth, 1966).

Kott, Jan, *Shakespeare our Contemporary*, tr. Boleslaw

Taborski (Methuen, London, 1964).

Lascelles, Mary, '*King Lear* and Doomsday', *Shakespeare Survey* 26 (1973); 69–79.

Levenson, Jill, 'What the Silence Said: Still Points in '*King Lear*', in Clifford Leech and J.M.R. Margeson (eds.) *Shakespeare 1971* (University of Toronto Press, Toronto and Buffalo, 1972, pp. 215–29).

Mack, Maynard, *King Lear in Our Time* (University of California Press, Berkeley and Los Angeles, 1965).

McLuskie, Kathleen, 'The Patriarchal Bard: Feminist Criticism and Shakespeare: *King Lear* and *Measure for Measure*', in Jonathan Dollimore and Alan Sinfield (eds.) *Political Shakespeare* (Manchester University Press, Manchester; and Cornell University Press, Ithaca and London, 1985), pp. 88–108.

Muir, Edwin, 'The Politics of *King Lear*', in *Essays on Literature and Society* (Hogarth Press, London, 1949), pp. 31 48.

Pirie, David, 'Lear as King', *Critical Quarterly* 22 (1980): 5–20.

Reibetanz, John, *The Lear World: A Study of King Lear in its Dramatic Context* (University of Toronto Press, Toronto and Buffalo, 1977).

Ribner, Irving, *Patterns in Shakespearian Tragedy* (Methuen, London, 1960).

Rosenberg, John D., 'King Lear and his Comforters', *Essays in Criticism* 16 (1966): 135–46.

Rosenberg, Marvin, *The Masks of King Lear* (University of California Press, Berkeley, Los Angeles and London, 1972).

Salgādo, Gāmini, *King Lear: Text and Performance* (Macmillan, London, 1984).

Shakespeare, William, *King Lear*, ed. Kenneth Muir (Arden edition; Methuen, London; and Harvard University Press, Massachusetts, 1952).

Skulsky, Harold, *Spirits Finely Touched* (University of Georgia Press, Athens, Georgia, 1976).

Sinfield, Alan, 'Lear and Laing', *Essays in Criticism* 26 (1976) 1–16.

Snyder, Susan, *The Comic Matrix of Shakespeare's Tragedies* (Princeton University Press, Princeton, 1979).

Snyder, Susan, 'King Lear and the Psychology of Dying', *Shakespeare Quarterly* 33 (1982) 449–60.

Stein, Walter, *Criticism as Dialogue* (Cambridge University Press, Cambridge, 1969).

Stewart, J.I.M., 'The Blinding of Gloster', *Review of English Studies* 21 (1945) 264–70.

Tate, Nahum, *The History of King Lear*, in Montague Summers (ed.), *Shakespeare Adaptions* (reprint Benjamin Blom, New York and London, 1966).

Taylor, Gary, and Warren, Michael (eds.), *The Division of the Kingdoms: Shakespeare's Two Versions of King Lear* (Clarendon Press, Oxford, 1983).

Traversi, Derek A., *An Approach to Shakespeare, 2: Troilus and Cressida to The Tempest*, 3rd edn (Hollis & Carter, London, 1969).

Urkowitz, Steven, *Shakespeare's Revision of King Lear* (Princeton University Press, Princeton, 1980).

Index